THE JOURNAL OF AN

ARMY SURGEON

DURING THE

PENINSULAR WAR

The Journal of an

Army Surgeon

during the

Peninsular War

by

CHARLES BOUTFLOWER

The Spellmount Library of Military History

SPELLMOUNT
Staplehurst

British Library Cataloguing in Publication Data:
A catalogue record for this book is available
from the British Library

Copyright © Spellmount Ltd 1997
Introduction © Dr Christopher Ticehurst 1997

ISBN 1-873376-85-5

First published in 1912
This edition first published in the UK in 1997
in
The Spellmount Library of Military History
by
Spellmount Ltd
The Old Rectory
Staplehurst
Kent TN12 0AZ

1 3 5 7 9 8 6 4 2

Printed in Great Britain by
T.J. Press (Padstow) Ltd
Padstow, Cornwall

AN INTRODUCTION
by Dr Christopher Ticehurst

In the early years of the 19th century the pay of an Army doctor was about four shillings a day, but a quarter of the income earned by a reasonably well respected doctor in civilian practice in England. Thus the Army tended to be cared for by doctors of poor quality: however there were some who joined for the adventure and it becomes clear from this journal that Dr Charles Boutflower was one of these. His journal covers the period from August 1809, just after the Battle of Talavera, through to May 1813 when the author was forced by illness to return to England, and so he missed the excitement of the great advances made in that year. Nonetheless in the four years he was with his beloved 40th Regiment in the Peninsula he covered a great deal of ground and was present, or nearby, at most of the set piece battles and sieges.

It is indeed his description of his movements which take up most of his narrative account and he passes over his medical work modestly; for example in early December 1809 he writes in a rather complaining vein: 'My time is so much engrossed by my professional duties that it is with difficulty that I can steal an hour now and then to keep up my communications with my friends in England.' It is a great joy to read of his campaign travels but it may be of value to have some inkling of his medical work which was after all his raison d'etre. This introduction is offered therefore as a brief summary of the professional involvement as a typical Regimental Surgeon in Wellington's Army at that time. First let us consider the man from what we know of him and from his views on various matters as expressed often vehemently in the pages of this book. Charles Boutflower was 19 years old when he joined the 40th Regiment in Malta. He had by this time obtained a degree from Edinburgh University. To qualify as a doctor at this age was by no means uncommon then, indeed he was probably older than most, though a great deal younger than the same achievement today. With his degree and with his upper middle class family background be would have been able to purchase a Commission and on joining his Regiment would have found one other doctor already there. Later on, at the time he rejoins his Regiment in 1809, he would have been in the company of two other Regimental Surgeons since in that year it became common practice to have three doctors with each regiment over 500 men on operational duty. This in itself is an indicator of the extent of the 'duties' involved in caring for the large numbers of sick men at all times and of the wounded in battle. The doctors were supported by Regimental Mates who might be doctors unable to afford a Commission but were most often soldiers taken out of field duties and given rudimentary training but who would be expected nonetheless to operate on the wounded under fire. Dr Boutflower gives us no hint of his relationships with his colleagues or with his Regimental Mates but we know from contemporaneous accounts that the latter group were most often of poor quality and holding only warrant rank could be dismissed without warning, imprisoned or even flogged.

As his Journal unfolds we find ourselves confronted with some colourful views on diverse matters. It is quite clear that he has a very low opinion of the Catholic Church in both Spain and Portugal and it is likely that these opinions were formed during his upbringing in an Anglican house but enhanced by observations on his travels, He has derogatory comments on Bishops (except at Guarda) and on 12th January 1810 is most scathing about a priest in Leyrosa who went straight to a gambling table from saying the last Mass on a Sunday. Soon after this, on 12th February 1810, his antipathy to monks and to nuns has reached such a pitch that he concludes that since Napoleon is 'annihilating' these Institutions it would be desirable that the French should eventually succeed in subjugating Spain and Portugal. This comment might be construed as a treason and so was probably kept within the leaves of his record and may find a reflection in the apologia with which he starts his account. Despite his views on the virtue of the nuns, he seems to have gained entrance to several Convents for various rather spurious reasons although he did visit at least some for the purpose of providing medical treatment. Women generally fare less well than the nuns and he criticises them for vulgarity in their speech and in their dress though he rates the Spanish women to be better by all accounts than those in Portugal. In general terms he has little good to write about Portugal and iterates the view that it was a dirty country including Lisbon itself. Lisbon comes in for harsh criticism towards the end of his diary when he is ill and waiting to board ship for England. It might be considered that these stern remarks are comparative to his views of England.

However there is no doubting the strength of his attack on a very Spanish affair – the bullfight. On the 5th October 1812 in Madrid he attended a bullfight and the following day writes at length about this horrific and barbarous spectacle which '. . . to a mind tinctured with the smallest degree of humanity cannot be witnessed without horror'.

We find in contrast, however, that he does not show much humanity after the successes through the breaches at Ciudad

Rodrigo and at Badajos, when he severely condemns the decision not to abide by the laws of war which would have led to the execution of the entire Garrisons for not surrendering once the breaches were made practicable.

Let us turn now to a consideration of Dr Boutflower's professional duties, and it is best dealt with by envisaging the medical problems of day-to-day existence on the move and in camp and then to move on to the additional surgical problems of treating the wounded in battle.

In medicine, there is an adage reminding the medical profession that commonest things are commonest and thus we may assume that much of Dr Boutflower's time was taken in treating infected throats and chest infections, which would be exacerbated by the soldiers having to march and even sleep in wet, sodden uniforms. Also common would be the intestinal upsets which might well be the result of drinking water contaminated by particles of debris – the so-called traveller's tummy – well enough known today. The four regiments joining the Army just before 6th August 1812 could well have been suffering from this simple but devastating bowel disturbance. However dysentery was also common enough and typhoid fever was a major problem in the summer months: whilst outbreaks of cholera were forever lurking, they seemed not to have created the havoc one might have thought likely. Heat exhaustion was clearly a serious problem and we find the Journal constantly making comment on the heat, particularly in July, August and September. Whilst the link between the ambient temperature and heat exhaustion was recorded it was clearly not understood that without rest, copious fluids and cooling, heat exhaustion leads on to heat stroke with fatal outcome. Malaria was endemic in the Iberian Peninsula at that time, as indeed it was in England, and was recognised by the remittent or intermittent fever coming every third or fourth day. Although Jesuit's bark, which contains quinine, had long since been used for the treatment of malaria, it was and is a devastating illness and such an infection struck Dr Boutflower at least three times during his service in Iberia, leading eventually to his evacuation to England on the orders of a medical board. Finally, we must remember that tuberculosis was a common condition and, in the absence of screening medical examination of recruits, might well have been present on arrival in the theatre of operations but aggravated by the heat would progress to severe and probably fatal dimension.

All of these problems would be treated initially in the Regimental Hospital, which was equipped to treat 60 cases (although it had only 12 beds). All of this equipment was carried on one bullock cart and the hospital set up at each resting place in a house or barn. Surgical instruments and medicines would have been carried on the doctor's own horse or his mule, all of which he was responsible for funding.

On an average day some 40% of the regiment would be sick, and we find in the Journal on 11th September 1811 that in the 40th Regiment 15 officers and some 600 men were ill. Earlier that year, writing near Badojos, Dr Boutflower has the foresight to write: 'I think it probable that in the course of the next six months we shall lose more men by sickness than by the sword.'

Whilst surgical problems did occur on quiet days, the main concerns would be the wounds caused in battle. Dr Boutflower reached Albuera on 17 May and declares: 'On our arrival on the Field of Combat a scene the most horrible that the imagination can conceive presented itself. The ground was covered with the dead and dying.' On the following day he continues: 'The wounded demanded the utmost care and in the event of such another day the loss of lives from the impossibility of giving proper attendance to all would have been very great indeed.' There is an inference here that some mode of sorting or triage was used and decisions made on who might be saved and those who could not.

Sabre cuts and penetrating lance wounds would usually be sewn together by the Regimental Mates using twine on unsterilised needles, hence they invariably became infected. The most severe wounds would be caused by high velocity fragments of metal from exploding shell and mines, and in siege situations by wood splinters also. The main cause of low velocity missile wounds at that time was musket balls.

Abdominal wounds would almost always prove fatal sooner or later, either from unstoppable haemorrhage or from peritonitis, and there was little the doctor could do. Chest wounds were not necessarily fatal if the missile missed the heart and the great blood vessels; Dr Boutflower would have learnt from experience that the fragment was best left alone in these circumstances. Head and face wounds were often survived provided that the medical staff could staunch the bleeding, though the disfigurement in the long term could be frightening.

Limb wounds were statistically the most common, and in the treatment of these Dr Boutflower would be much involved. The problem here is that the wound is caused by the transfer of energy from the missile (the musket ball) to the limb and the impact force produces dead muscle and in this dead muscle will grow bacteria responsible for tetanus and gas gangrene. These bacteria, which live in the bowels of all animals with no untoward effect, grow exponentially in dead muscle and the toxic effect of this is invariably fatal. Whereas today, and in good measure since the introduction of antisepsis and anaesthetics, dead muscle can be surgically removed and the wound left clean, this was not possible in the Napoleonic period; the requirement to amputate all wounded limbs was seen as an imperative life saving measure.

We know from other accounts that Wellington was concerned over the health of his troops, if only because he had the need to conserve manpower. Although Dr Boutflower mentions W often enough in his Journal, he does not explain how this concern was made manifest, nor, sadly, does he relate to us his relationship with the Commanding Officer of the 40th Regiment. There is little for the medical reader to glean about the overall medical direction in these four years, but it is of interest that in the last few days he becomes involved with the Inspector of Hospitals (McGrigor) and with the senior surgeon (Guthrie), both of whom were to achieve eminent positions and reputations in England after 1815.

It is a pity that this Journal and the good doctor's active service both ended prematurely with his own medical evacuation to England. Almost certainly one feels he was brought down not by the malaria alone but from exhaustion through attention to his 'duties'.

Dr Christopher Ticehurst
1997

PREFACE.

THE following pages contain the Journal kept by the late Charles Boutflower, Surgeon to the 40th (then the 2nd Somersetshire and now South Lancashire) Regiment, during the Peninsular War.

It has been considered better to print the Journal exactly as it was written, and any reader who might feel inclined to take offence at the views of the author will kindly bear in mind that it was written over a hundred years ago : and that any passages which might at the present date be deemed better expunged merely express the individual views of the writer at that remote date.

The reader will notice that the Journal opens up with an apology by the author which he will no doubt bear in mind.

The Journal has been printed by the author's relatives from the original by the permission of the Revd. Douglas S. Boutflower, of Christ Church, Sunderland, in whose possession the Journal now is.

JOURNAL.

Haec olim Meminisse Juvabit.

A S this Journal is undertaken at the request of one or two very dear Friends, and as it will certainly never come under the inspection of many others, I trust they will deem this some Apology for the Egotisms that will naturally prevail in it.

On the 10th August, 1809, I embarked on Board the Thomas Transport in order to join the 40th Regiment with Sir Arthur Wellesly.   It was intended we should sail the following Morning, but the wind getting round to the westward prevented us.   In the course of the 11th was introduced to Capn. Rodney, of H.M.S. Fylla, under Orders for Lisbon with Money. Capn. R. very politely offered me a Passage. An offer so agreeable I immediately availed myself of, and lost no time in removing my Luggage from the Thomas to the Fylla.   I had particular pleasure in bidding adieu to the former Vessel, as, besides the inconvenience naturally resulting from her smallness, the Officers on board her were from what I could ascertain in so very short a period generally exceptionable.   Very strong westerly winds prevented our sailing till the 15th, on which day we received the particulars of the Memorable Battle of Talavera.   It was a source of some regret to us that we could not convey to our friends in Spain & Portugal an account of the Capture of Flushing. On this day I recollected that my dear & revered Father completed his seventy-third Year, and, while I offered up a Prayer to the Almighty that his valuable Life might yet be spared to his Family and Friends, I had a sensation of severe pain originating in the idea that from his advanced age I should never see him more.   Having been now three days on board the Fylla I had an opportunity of observing the several characters of those who were to form my Society for the next Week or ten Days. Prior to my introduction to Capn. Rodney, he had received into his Cabin as many as he could conveniently accommodate ; it was therefore necessary that I should take my Passage in the Gun Room with the Officers of the Ship. The day subsequent to Capn. R.'s offer I had the good fortune to be particularly introduced to the Second Lieutenant,from whom in consequence I received the most marked attention.

Capn. R. is the son of the celebrated Lord Rodney. He is six and twenty years of age, and has been at Sea almost from his infancy ; he appears very fond of his profession, and certainly is remarkably attentive to everything that relates to the safety of the Ship, arising less, I believe, from any personal fear of danger, than from a due Sense of the serious responsibility that attaches to the Situation of a Captain of a Man of War. His Education, from a reason above stated, has been much neglected, added to which his Talents are certainly not above Mediocrity. His disposition, however, is very good, and I should certainly form an unfavourable Opinion of an Officer who could not live pleasantly under his Command. Capn. R. had two Gentlemen with him in his Cabin, one of them Brigr. Genl. Madden going out to command a Brigade of Portuguese Troops. He was formerly Major of the 12th Dragns., and served with them in Egypt, but was subsequently dismissed the Service, by the Sentence of a General Court Martial ; tho' the crimes were undoubtedly a breach of Military Discipline, it does not appear that his reputation either as an Officer or Gentleman suffered in consequence, having been since almost constantly employed in England as an Inspecting Field Officer, and in his present employment he is evidently thought worthy of a high command. He is a Man of superior Abilities, and possesses a general knowledge of Men and Manners. He has visited more than once almost every Court in Europe, &, having a perfect knowledge of nearly all the modern languages, he has been enabled to form more accurate conclusions of what came

under his observation than the generality of those who travel.
From his conversation, of which I very much availed myself
during the Passage, I derived both information and amusement.
The only other Passenger in the Cabin was a Mr. Vanzeleer,
who may justly be styled a " vrai-Portugues," being possessed
of all the prejudice which so eminently distinguishes that
Nation. He had come to England for the purpose of investing
a considerable sum of money in the English Funds, justly
considering that every species of property is become very
unsafe in Portugal. He had been six months in England,
and, never having been out of his own Country before, anyone
would have naturally supposed that he would have been both
astonished and delighted with what he had seen, as, according
to his own account, he had visited everything worth seeing in
London and its environs, but on the contrary nothing
appeared to have pleased him. Prejudiced, as he certainly is,
I verily believe that Envy had no small share in the dissatis-
faction he constantly expressed when speaking of England.
A Portuguese who has never travelled thinks there is nothing
in the world equal to Lisbon; disappointed, however, on arriving
in other Countries to find that he has been all his Life mistaken,
he has not ingenuousness sufficient to avow what it is impossible but he must be so well acquainted with.

Our Number in the Gun Room consisted of seven ; namely,
two Lieutenants, the Purser, Lieutenant of Marines, a Young
Gentleman going out as a Volunteer to General Beresford, the
Surgeon of the Ship, and myself. To the whole of the Officers
I feel indebted for their attentions, and particularly to the
2d Lieutenant, to whom, as I before stated, I had the good
fortune to be particularly introduced. This Officer possesses
a highly cultivated Mind, and has so great a taste for reading,
that during the whole Passage when not on duty I scarcely
once observed him without a Book in his hand. His Library
consisted of upwards of three hundred Volumes of the most
approved Authors in the English, French, Spanish, & Italian
Languages, of all of which he has attained considerable know-

8

ledge. His disposition appears to be naturally of the sombre cast, tho' the recent death of his Father may probably have given it that turn. We passed many hours in conversation together, and he succeeded so completely in gaining my esteem and regard that it was with much reluctance I bade him adieu. Good fortune will, I trust, bring us together again, when I shall renew my intimacy with him with unfeigned pleasure.

On the 16th while beating down Channel saw H.M.S. Argo with Convoy from the West Indies. From a recollection of my own Sensations on former occasions I had an idea of the happiness they were enjoying on being so near their Native Shore.

17th. Fired two shots at a strange Sail to bring her to. She proved to be a Revenue Cutter from Guernsey on a Cruise. The Master of her came on board the Fylla, and, his manner being such as gave Capn. Rodney great offence, much altercation ensued. Capn. R. at length let him go, previously writing across his Warrant an account of his disrespectful Conduct for the information of any other Captain of a Man-[of-war] who might board him.

On the 18th, notwithstanding the continuous contrary winds, we found ourselves at 9 a.m. off the Lizard. In the afternoon were boarded by a Fishing Boat belonging to Mount's Bay, which not only supplied us with fresh Fish for Dinner, but was also the bearer of some Letters ashore. I availed myself of this opportunity to write to my inestimable friend Mrs. B. At dusk the same Evening I lost sight of the Land's End. How torpid the Bosom, and how unworthy the name of Britain must he be, who can quit his country without offering up a fervent Prayer for its welfare. In taking a last look of its fading shores a variety of Sensations occupied my Mind, some of them painful; but I think the contrary predominated. A thousand instances of its many blessings and general Superiority over other Nations rushed upon my recollection, and it was not without a feeling of conscious pride that I called myself an Englishman. The night proved stormy, and I suffered much from sea-sickness till the morning of the 21st. It is somewhat strange that my susceptibility for that Complaint appears to increase with each succeeding voyage I make. On the 20th we chased a ship under suspicious circumstances. Prize Money was the Order of the Day. On coming up with her, however, she proved to be a Merchant Man from London bound to Malta. She ran from us under the idea that we were a French Privateer.

The wind still continued contrary. On the 23rd we made Cape Finisterre, but were so far in the Bay that we found it impossible to weather it. We were consequently obliged to tack and stand out to Sea. In the Afternoon the wind fortunately shifted sufficiently to enable our getting round it.

On the 24th run down the coast of Spain, passing Vigo and the River Minho, which divides that country from Portugal. 25th, had the wind fair but little of it; in the Afternoon came in site of the Burlings, Rocks perfectly well known to all who have navigated this Coast. The wind freshening this Evening gave us every hope of being in Lisbon the following Morning about eleven. At night being in the Latitude of Lisbon we lay to till Daylight the following Morning, when we again got under weigh, and stood in shore; having to beat up the Tagus it was twelve o'clock before we came to an Anchor, having had a Passage of eleven Days, and, with the exception of the two or three Days' bad weather, to me as pleasant a one as anything could be in a Ship. During our voyage I read Mdme. De Stael Holstein's Corinna in the Original, and also Robertson's History of the Reign of Charles V. The former is doubtless a work of considerable ability; to the story the Authoress has very happily added an Acct. of the chief Paintings, Sculpture, & other Works of Art, at present remaining in Italy, which, at the same time it appears to say everything necessary on the Subject, never fatigues by saying more than is necessary. The characters of Lord Nelvil and

Corinna are finely drawn and are perhaps faithful delineations of the difference existing in the two Nations. In writing this work however I think an Englishwoman would not have tarnished so many good Qualities (as Madame S. bestowed on Lord N.), by his unpardonable, and as appears to me his unjustifiable, inconstancy. The Character of Lucilia is in my opinion highly natural. Of the latter work, there has never been any difference of Sentiment as to the Ability with which it is written. Most People in reading it, however they may admire the Political ingenuity and the firmness with which he (Charles) carried into effect everything likely to conduce to the great objects of his Ambition, will I doubt not feel more interested for his less fortunate but certainly more principled Rival, Francis, the King of France; the subtle cunning & perfidy of Charles form a striking contrast to the open and unsuspicious disposition of Francis, and whatever the former may gain of our Admiration, the latter has the Superior Merit of commanding our Esteem. The Spanish Monarch to me never appeared so dignified and great, as when cultivating his garden at his retirement at Saint Just, and I closed his History, fully determined, if possible, to visit that celebrated spot during my sojourn in Spain.

From the entrance of the Tagus to Lisbon is a distance of about fifteen Miles; being obliged to beat up gave us an opportunity of more particularly observing both Shores. That on the right side furnishes little worthy of note. The left, or Lisbon side, presents a beautiful and diversified prospect, chiefly consisting of the Country Seats of the Queen, Prince Regent, and Nobility. The principal Forts in the Tagus are first a large Tower, intended as a State Prison, which stands in the centre of the River; higher up on the left is Fort St. Julian; and still higher on the same side is Belem Castle. At Belem Lisbon may be said to commence, notwithstanding the City is called three miles from it. Where Belem terminates, Buenos Ayres, (so called from its high & supposed healthy situation) begins, and again at the end of Buenos Ayres is the commencement of the City of Lisbon. The whole being built of white stone, and standing on the Side of a Hill, presents a pleasing *coup d'oeil*, and promises the newly arrived stranger more gratification from the expectation of visiting it than he afterwards realises. After being an hour or two at Anchor I went ashore for the purpose of delivering a Letter from my Friend Capn. B. to a Mr. Kennedy, the Agent Victualler. On arriving in Lisbon, opposite to which we had brought up, I found that Mr. K. resided at Belem. I had in consequence to walk (as I have before stated) a distance of three miles, and nearly the length of the whole Town. This walk gave me a disgust of the place I have never since been able to overcome; tho' in some degree prepared to expect a City not remarkable for its cleanliness, I had never formed an idea that a Metropolis could be so abominably filthy. I shall not enter into a description of it, but shall content myself by stating that the impression made upon one of my senses was such as I shall not easily forget.

From Mr. Kennedy I received a most polite and kind attention, and had the pleasure a day or two after to meet at his House at Dinner, a very old Friend, Capn. H. of the Navy, the principal agent for Transports in the Tagus. Having much the same idea of Lisbon as myself he had very wisely fitted up his Cabin most comfortably and constantly resided aboard. He gave me a most pressing invitation to remain with him during the few Days I should stay at Lisbon, an offer so concordant to my wishes that I most gladly availed myself of it. I had not yet quitted the Fylla, but, as she was ordered to be in readiness to proceed to England, I lost no time in removing my things from her.

The day after my arrival I waited on the Commandant, who informed me that it would be necessary for me to proceed to join my Regiment with as little delay as possible, adding that he believed I should find them at Elvas, a fortified Town on the Frontier. Great was my disappointment when I understood that the Victory at

[1809]
[AUGUST] Talavera had not been followed by more happy Consequences. I had fully expected to have joined the Army at Madrid, elated with hope and flushed with victory. On the contrary I found that they were depressed by Famine and Sickness, and in full march to the Frontiers of Portugal. This reverse was owing to two Causes : the neglect of the Spanish Commissariat in not furnishing Provisions, and the inability not to say worse of Cuesta. Fortunately for his country this General solicited his resignation, a request which the Junta appears very readily to have complied with.

[SEPT.] I remained in Lisbon, or rather in the Tagus, till the 3rd September. The oppressive state of the weather prevented me from paying that attention to its Curiosities I otherwise should. The Aqueduct, which is certainly the principal, I only saw from a distance ; the theatres I never visited. The Convent of San Jeronymo I found worthy of attention ; it is an immense building and is calculated to afford a high treat to the Lovers of Architecture ; it contains some fine paintings by some of the most esteemed Masters, and a very good Library. On the 3rd in the evening I crossed the Tagus to Aldea Gallega, a small town nearly opposite to Lisbon, and about fifteen miles over. This place furnishes nothing worthy of remark, being a small and dirty Town. I had much difficulty in procuring a Billet; indeed I found the People generally more uncivil here than in any other place. Having procured a Couple of Mules I set forward on my Journey the Afternoon of the 5th, intending to sleep that Night at a Village called Pegoens. On my arrival there however I found it so extremely miserable and so entirely devoid of every species of accommodation, that I determined to proceed to another village, Vendas Novas, three Leagues further, eight Leagues or thirty two miles from Aldea Gallega, a Portuguese League being fully equal to four English miles. It was late when I reached Vendas Novas. The Inn however afforded some bad Chocolate and a miserable Bed in a more miserable Room. At an early hour the following morning I set off for Montemoro Novo three leagues further. On my way I met Col. Stibball of the Guards, who first informed me of the 40th being in Badajos. Just as I entered this Town it commenced a heavy Rain, which I feared would detain me all that Day, and prevent my reaching Elvas the following; fortunately however it cleared up in the afternoon, and enabled me to proceed to Arreiolis that evening. Montemoro Novo is a pretty Town of some extent. It stands very high, and is fortified. The accommodation however in the Inn was little better than at Vendas Novas. Arreiolis is a miserable place three Leagues distant from Montemoro. My Bed looked tolerably clean, but before the Morning I was nearly eat up in it; the irritation I suffered nearly threw me into a fever. Early the next Day, being the 7th of the Month, I set off for Estremos, six Leagues further on the Road. Half way is an Inn called Venda de Duque where I stopped to refresh my Mule and get myself Breakfast. While there, an Officer of the 40th entered on his way to Lisbon, from whom I collected all the news of the Regiment. I reached Estremos in the Afternoon, and found to my satisfaction a very good Inn, and where everything comfortable was to be procured. It is well fortified and stands upon a high Hill. There is a certain cleanliness in its appearance not to be met with in any other Town I saw in Portugal. Indeed were I compelled to live in that Country I think I should select Estremos as my place of residence.

On the 8th, in the Morning I recommenced my Journey for Elvas, being six leagues further and twenty-seven from Aldea Gallega. I had the satisfaction of reaching it early in the Afternoon, after having travelled over an hundred and four Miles, evincing not the smallest Vestige of Cultivation excepting in the immediate Vicinity of the different Towns. At Elvas I remained till the 10th, to enable my Servant to come up, having left him behind on the Road. I had the good fortune here to meet with a Doctor Deane, Physician to the Forces, brother to Capn. Deane of the 96th Regiment, with whom I had always lived on terms of the greatest intimacy. From Dr. Deane I experienced the most gratifying attentions, indeed he received me with a kindness I have rarely experienced on a first introduction. Elvas has long been celebrated for its great strength, or rather the Fort which commands it known by the Name of La Lippe, which is justly considered one of the most impregnable Fortifications in the world. The Aqueduct here also is a very singular Structure on an immense scale. The water is conveyed by it to the Town over a very uneven Surface for the distance of nearly a Mile. The Town itself stands high, and is remarkably strong. Like the generality of Portuguese Towns however it is filthy in the extreme, so much so that I sincerely congratulated myself I was not going to remain in it. The Convents I found generally filled with the Sick of our Army, and the numbers were truly afflicting.

From Elvas Badajos may be most distinctly seen, and it appears to be very near; they are distant however at least twelve Miles. On the 10th I proceeded to Badajos, where I met with many of my old Friends in the 40th. The short time I had been absent from them had produced great changes, as I perceived a variety of new faces. Badajos is the Capital of the Province of Estremadura, situated on the River Guadiana, over which you pass by a Bridge of twenty-one Arches, as you enter the town from Elvas. The two Countries are separated by a Branch of this River, which is nearly dry in the Summer, and is distant about four miles from Badajos on the Elvas road. The difference between the two people at this short distance is remarkable; there is such a jealousy and even hatred existing between them, that each carefully avoids imitating the Manners and Customs of the other. On entering Badajos I was much pleased to find an air of cleanliness superior to anything I had observed in Portugal. What most particularly struck me was the vast superiority that the Spanish Women have over the Portuguese in Person, Air, Appearance, and Dress. The latter are in general very slovenly, while the former are particularly neat in their modes of dress, and have an inexpressible elegance and dignity in their walk which I have never seen in any other women.

I found everything very uncertain relative to our future Movements, every Person enjoying their own private opinions. This place was Head-Quarters, Lord Wellington and the Heads of Departments residing here. The 40th Regiment the only one here, the Army being stationed in various Quarters in the different Towns in the Neighbourhood in such a manner that the whole might unite in one Day in Case of necessity.

On the 12th an opportunity presented itself of writing to England by a Friend, of which I availed myself. Weather dreadfully hot, scarcely to be borne, even by the Inhabitants who dread it much. This Month has ever been considered here as the most unhealthy in the Year. It has given rise to an old Spanish proverb, that whoever lives out September may expect to live another Year. Diseases generally predominating are Fevers and Intermittents.

[Oct.]

The 1st October.—Accts. reach us from England of the intended change of Ministers. Much anxiety of course on the part of Lord Wellington ; indeed a general interest on the occasion by all parties, as our remaining here very probably depends on the Sentiments of those who may assume the Reins of Government.

8th. Lord W. quitted Badajos for Lisbon, supposed in great measure for the purpose of being enabled sooner to receive accts. from England. The Day preceding he gave a Dinner to a Number of Spaniards of both Sexes, and in the Evening a Ball to the Garrison which was crowded almost to suffocation. I was much pleased with his manner.

In the midst of a variety of Reports that the Army was immediately to advance towards Lisbon for the purpose of embarking for England, on the 9th the 3d Batt. 27th Regt. marched in here from Lisbon, which gave rise to the idea that we are as certainly to remain. From undoubted authority I heard that a Voluminous Report of the state of the country by the Marquis Wellesly and on which everything was likely to depend, after having been perused by Lord Wellington, was forwarded from here on the 19th ulto.

[1809]
[Oct.] On the 10th came in here to be quartered two Battalions of the Guards, making the Garrison to consist of four Regts. besides Artillery, & the difficulty of getting billets was so great that very serious remonstrances were obliged to be made to the Junta on the occasion, who in their turn threatened the Inhabitants with severe pains and penalties if they made any unnecessary obstruction to the accommodation of British Officers. They are evidently getting tired of us, and, tho' they have no objection to our fighting for them, they would wish the Troops to remain in the Fields during the Winter ; some of them are so extremely uncivil that nothing will be sufficient but the entrance of French Troops into their Houses to convince them of their ingratitude.

I write this on the 22d. October, having hitherto been unable to keep a regular Journal. What I have written is chiefly from Memory aided by a very few Notes. Sickness has constantly prevailed in the Army to an alarming extent, there being seldom less than eight thousand sick on an average, of which number the Deaths have been most afflicting. The Weather still continues very hot, but the Mornings and Evenings are extremely pleasant. Lord Wellington returns this Day from Lisbon, when it is probable we may learn something of the intended future arrangements ; as yet we are entirely ignorant of the State of the Continent. An Officer who came here a few days since from the French Head-Quarters states, that he was informed by the French Commandant that Peace with Austria was actually signed. Should such be the case, I think there can be no doubt but we should evacuate the Peninsula. It would be absurd in the extreme to attempt with our Numbers to oppose the undivided force of France. The Spaniards are apprehensive we shall leave them, but speak with confidence of bringing the Contest to a happy issue. For my own part I have no doubt that the French will possess all the principal Towns and Fortresses in the Kingdom, but I feel certain that they will never have undisturbed possession of them ; insurrections will constantly prevail wherever the French are not in force, and that irreconcileable hatred & detestation the Spaniards have for the French will induce them to murder them whenever they can possibly effect it.

Octr. 24. Lord Wellington did not return on the 22d. as was expected. He is still detained at Lisbon, but on what account we know not.

Yesterday I had the satisfaction of receiving several Letters from England, a satisfaction only to be appreciated by those who are abroad like myself, and who possess Friends so valuable as mine are.

This Day War was proclaimed with the usual formalities in the principal Streets against Denmark. The political events likely to originate from this Circumstance are, I conceive, very small.

27th. Letters were received this Morning from Lord W. stating his intention of being here on the 29th Inst. It is certain he has been visiting various Situations in Portugal, from which it is inferred that he is about to take up positions for the defence of that Country. In the meantime we go on in the old way, continually inundated with reports which all in the end prove equally fallacious. The most Credulous I believe are now become suspecting, and even official Accounts are received with distrust.

There is certainly a general wish throughout the Army that we may soon be ordered to England, and I am sorry to observe that near nine out of ten of all the Officers I have conversed with on the subject would hail the News of Peace being concluded between Austria and France, provided it led to that event. For my own part I have no wish to quit this Country. The weather is getting pleasanter and the number of the Sick is consequently decreasing. Time so far from hanging heavy, as most complain, appears to me to fly with unprecedented rapidity. It is true the Amusements are limited, but Duty, Books and Riding amply suffice to fill up every hour. In the Evening there is at the House of one of the principal Families here a Conversazione, or as it is termed in the language of this

Country a Pertiglia. Hither the principal Persons of both Sexes resort, and also as many British Officers as are disposed, but as the Spanish Language is known to very few of them, and, as without that knowledge these parties are certainly very stupid, in general there are not many English Officers there. When not otherwise engaged, I generally look in ; and I find that it is a very good plan to adopt in order to improve in the language. My frequent Visits, which have afforded me an opportunity of becoming acquainted with many of the Ladies of this place, have confirmed me in the superiority I have always attached to my own fair Countrywomen over all others. From habit and bad example the women here even of the first rank have contracted an indelicacy in their ideas and conversation which would shock the most abandoned in England. Indeed public Morals in general in this Country in both Sexes are at a very low ebb, and yet in no part of the world perhaps are the forms of Religion more strictly adhered to. The Bells are constantly ringing for Church, into which crowds are as constantly entering. In the Houses of every Family you will continually hear long prayers. In the Streets even you will always observe some mark or other of Devotion. How is it then that such general licentiousness, so many thefts, &c. &c. prevail ? Doubtless because though they have the form of Religion they possess not the Spirit ; and for my own part I need no other proof of the fallacy and Error of the Romish Church than the conviction forced upon my mind by the Lives and Conduct of its Votaries, that it is not a Religion of the Heart. A Religious Mind cannot but feel shocked at the profane manner in which the Sabbath is observed here. It is not sufficient that Amusements are partaken of in the same manner as on other Days. Sunday is always selected as a Day on which they are pursued with unusual avidity. Neither is working, buying or selling generally abstained from. When witnessing their solemn Mummeries of a Sunday Morning during the Celebrations of Mass, with their Priests, decked out like those of Baal, performing a number of Mystical Ceremonies in the midst of Frankincense and lighted Candles, the idea of their subsequent Mode of passing the Sabbath occurs to my recollection, and I involuntarily exclaim with the Apostle— " Be not deceived ; God is not mocked."

Badajos furnishes nothing particularly worthy of observation. It abounds with Churches, and has five Convents for Friars and nine for Nuns. The Cathedral is a handsome building and has three Organs. It is profusely hung with Crimson Velvet edged with Gold Lace; in one part is affixed a List of Books prohibited to be read by the Inquisition under pain of several severe Penalties ; among others I observed the letters of Lord Chesterfield and also those of Lady Mary Wortley Montague; the Religious Works of the celebrated Neckar are also among them.

Octr. 30   Lord Wellington returned last Night, but if he brings any News it has not yet transpired.   We are now a long time without Accounts from England ; from whence we infer that the News brought from Talavera by Captn. Gordon relative to the Peace between Austria and France is not true, though it was published as Official in General Orders at the French Head-Quarters.   On the 2d. of next month Lord Wellington goes to Seville for a few days in order to have an interview with his Brother the Marquis.   Doubtless a variety of opinions will be the consequence of his undertaking this second Expedition.   Seville is distant from Badajos about one hundred and twenty miles.

[Nov.]   November. In consequence of a subsequent Arrangement Lord Wellington quitted us this Morning for Seville, instead of to-morrow, as was his intention. He has left an order behind him which has considerably annoyed us ; viz., for the 40th Regiment to march on the 3d. Inst. to Olivenza, a small town about four leagues distant from hence. Having formed an acquaintance with several of the most pleasant Families, we were enabled to pass our Evenings agreeably. Olivenza, I hear, does not abound with many of these Houses, and the difficulty and trouble of getting acquainted with those few is also to be surmounted. Another reason why I most prefer the place we are now in is its being Head-Quarters, by which means we get the earliest intelligence of any News there may be stirring.

This being the day of All Saints has been observed here with much Solemnity. About eight in the morning I was attracted into the Convent of the Catalans by the sound of Female Voices. On entering I observed a great many women kneeling before an Altar, and really singing with considerable sweetness; soon after the Nuns entered a chapel behind, grated off from the Church, where mass is performed. As they brought in several Lights, I had an opportunity of observing their Countenances, and to my surprise I found that they were all very old women, not one of them appearing less than sixty. They seemed to be about thirty or forty in number. They performed their devotions with considerable energy assisted by a miserable old Spinnet. Several British Officers were earnestly looking thro' the bars of the grating, which did not at all appear to attract their attention. About nine High Mass was performed in the Cathedral, at which a great concourse of People attended of both Sexes. The Music consisted of a fine toned organ with several Violins & other Instruments. There was the usual Chorus assisted by some very good lay singers hired for the purpose. The selection was chiefly from Pleyel, & was really very well executed; I was much pleased with it. After Mass a Sermon was preached; my knowledge of the language was just sufficient to enable me to understand that after dwelling on the Holiness of the Saints the Preacher exhorted all to imitate them, reminding his Hearers that they had the same assistance from above, and had no greater difficulties or Passions to contend with than those whose sanctity he was recommending them to imitate. During the Service I observed much laughing & other marks of indevotion among the People, and from which the Priests themselves were by no means free.

Novr. 8. In obedience to orders we marched to

this place (Olivenza) on the 3d. Inst. It is a neat Town formerly belonging to the Portuguese, but ceded to the Spaniards in the Peace of 1801. The inhabitants are nearly all Portuguese, and the hatred I have before mentioned to exist between the two People is here at its height. The Garrison consists of five Regiments besides Dragoons and Artillery, the whole under the command of the Honble. Majr. Genl. Cole. We are still without any accounts from England; in consequence great fears are entertained for the safety of the Packet. The news from Lisbon reports that Buonaparté is dangerously ill at Vienna, and that the Armistice is in consequence prolonged.

11th. The arrival of English papers of the 27th Ulto. has served to set at issue the thousand Reports and Rumours we have been lately inundated with. There appears little doubt that Peace between Austria and France is concluded, and yet the Accounts of it in the English Papers as copied from the Continental ones do not appear to be of such unequivocal testimony as to demand our unqualified belief. Unfortunately however as there is too much reason to give Credence to it, everyone is supposing what will be the Instructions to Lord Wellington in consequence. All are agreed that we must immediately evacuate the Peninsula, but the Opinions as to where the Army may afterwards be ordered are innumerable. It is very probable that the strongest Regiments will not return to England. Among these is the 40th, who are still very effective. It is however impossible to form an idea of the intentions of Government on this subject. I should not have the smallest objection to go up the Mediterranean ; indeed I feel no objection to go to any part of the world, the West Indies alone excepted.

The Accounts of Peace will doubtless considerably dishearten the Spaniards, tho' I believe they pretty generally anticipate that such a circumstance will compel us to withdraw our personal assistance.

Lord Wellington was to arrive at Badajos from Seville last Night. It is said that the Packet has brought out to him

Dispatches of the utmost importance, which may possibly determine the point in question. It is difficult to form an idea of what will be the Sentiments of the Spaniards, if we quit the Country; whether vexation and discontent for our not remaining to do more will not prevail over the gratitude they ought to feel for what we have already done. I should be sorry to think anything should beget an Animosity towards us from a People I think generally disposed to admire and esteem the English Character. It is, I believe, well ascertained that, in the different wars between England and Spain, and when the latter Country was in the closest alliance with France, an Englishman was always received with an Attention and marked Regard by the Spaniards which they never could testify towards a Frenchman ; and as a proof of the high estimation Spain has always considered an alliance with England, there is an old Spanish proverb which runs thus ;— "Paz con Inglaterra Y con todo el Mondo Guerra," which simply means, " Peace with England, and war with all the world."

25th. Nothing particular has occurred since the last Date. There has certainly been an action in La Mancha between the French & Spanish Armies, but the result is not correctly known. Lord Wellington is at present on a shooting expedition. He has the whole of his Baggage with him, in order, it is supposed, that when he proposes moving to a greater distance it may not be suspected. There is a general rumour that the Army is about to move, but it does not appear to rest on any solid foundation.

The weather from being intensely cold has become extremely pleasant. The Sickness in the Garrison has been and indeed still is very alarming. The number of Sick is not less than five hundred in this place alone.

28th. Certain Accounts have reached this place of the result of the action in La Mancha. The Spaniards in killed, wounded and Prisoners have not lost less than 20,000 Men, and it appears that the remainder of their Army is nearly dispersed.

By the arrival of the newspapers to the 15th Inst., and Accts. from apparently good Authority it seems that Ministers have determined on defending Portugal. How long we shall be able to maintain ourselves, particularly since the defeat of the Spaniards, remains to be proved. There are various opinions on the subject ; that we shall ultimately be compelled to quit, I think admits of little doubt, tho' probably the approaching Season, and the difficulty of procuring Supplies may prevent the Enemy from annoying us for some time.

[DEC.]   December 2d. The Spaniards do not seem to be the least dispirited at the result of the late Battle—on the contrary it appears to have roused them to fresh exertions. They deny that it was so disastrous as has been represented, and tho' they acknowledge to have lost an immense Number of Men they affirm that the loss of the French was also very great. The Marquis de la Romana is stated to have taken the Command of the La Mancha Army, and it is said that the first act of his power was the hanging of five Colonels, whether for Treason or Cowardice I have not heard. Gerona continues to hold out; and I was a few days ago assured by one of the principal Inhabitants of this place, in a manner and with a solemnity which evinced his own Credence of what he was relating, that the protracted defence of Gerona and the inability of the Enemy to conquer it were owing to the intercession of a Bishop who lived there about sixteen centuries since, and who from his uncommon Piety was justly ranked among the most eminent Saints this country had produced. He also informed me that he (my informer) was a Native of Gerona, and that he has now four Brothers residing there who have witnessed the Bishop appearing among them and stimulating them to additional exertions. He added his firm belief that Saragossa had held out so long by the aid afforded by our Lady of Pilar, tho' he could not explain how she had at length lost her interest. He was much shocked at my doubting that she had never possessed it.

On quitting the 96th Regiment I made a promise to a Captn. Deane in it with whom I had been particularly intimate to find out if possible a Brother of his serving in this Country as Physician to the Forces. On arriving at Lisbon, I enquired for him and was informed he was at Elvas. On reaching the latter place I soon found him out, and on making myself known to him was received with a kindness and warmth I had scarcely ever before experiencéd. I remained with him two Days during which short time from a Congeniality of Sentiment we became more intimately acquainted than is usual in so short a period. The urgent duties of war prevented us seeing one another so often as we wished. We continued however to pay reciprocal visits once a fortnight, the distance from Elvas to Badajos being not more than twelve miles. On my removal to this place it became totally out of my power to visit Elvas any more, and Dr. Deane from being equally engaged was unable to come over to Olivenza. A few days since, having occasion to send to Elvas, I wrote a Note to my Friend, and was horror-struck on the return of the Bearer to find that he was no more. He informed me that on reaching Elvas he found poor Deane very ill; that on the note being presented to him he attempted to read it but failed. He expired the following Morning, and with him as much worth as I ever knew in any individual. He was about twenty-eight years of age, intelligent in his Profession, irreproachable in conduct, and of an excellent disposition. His Physiognomy was most pleasing. His Forehead and Eyes reminded me strongly of an highly valued Friend I possess in England. While living he had engaged the esteem of all who had the happiness of his acquaintance, and since his Death the sorrow expressed for his loss loudly testifies the worth and value of his character.

The weather is now most delightful, but the People here seem much surprised that the Rainy Season has not set in some time. Sickness still prevails in the Garrison & indeed generally throughout the Army. My time is so much engrossed by my professional duties that it is with difficulty I can steal an hour now and then to keep up my communications with my Friends in England.

5th. A continuance of fine weather has had a most happy effect on my Sick. Those in Hospital are getting considerably better, and those out keep well. I have in consequence much less to do at present than I have had since my Arrival in this Country. I am now enabled to take long rides into the Neighbourhood, and was yesterday much gratified to find myself in a really neat and very pretty Village. It is called St. George, and has an appearance of Health, Happiness and Contentment I have seldom witnessed. It consists of two narrow Streets. Vines are made to grow over from the houses on one side to those opposite,which in the Summer most completely exclude the Rays of the Sun. There is a general Cleanliness in the whole Village which I have not before observed in this Country.

There is a certain bustle at Head-Quarters, and some preparations are making which in the opinion of many indicate a speedy Movement. If we are about to march it is devoutly to be wished it may be before the setting in of the bad Weather.

I had an opportunity this Afternoon of witnessing the Funeral of a Person of property. The procession consisted of the different Orders of Clergy & Friars and the male Friends of the deceased in great Numbers. The Body was conveyed in a sort of half Coffin, and was dressed in the Clothes that the deceased was in the habit of wearing when alive. During the procession there was a general Clatter of the Bells, producing the most inharmonious discord, so much that an Italian with a fine ear would have envied the Defunct his inability of hearing them. On entering the Church the Corpse was placed on a Table, when the friends arranged themselves around it, each bearing a large wax Candle. A solemn Mass is next chaunted, in which the intercession of the Virgin Mary is frequently invoked. This Mass performed they move to the Grave where the Corpse is deposited, and a Napkin being thrown over the

Face the Dirt is thrown in. A similar Mass is again performed which finishes the Service. Rich and Poor are all buried within the Churches; only the wealthy however are permitted to lie near the Altar. It is never the custom to put a deceased person into a Coffin in the mode we do in England. Both Sexes are neatly dressed on their Death, and placed in a half Coffin from which they are never moved. Children are frequently put into the ground without any envelope.

9th. From the general orders of this Day, conjecture as to moving is at an end. The Guards marched this morning from Badajos, and the different Divisions of the Army are to follow in succession. Speculation is however considerably excited as to our destination, which is kept profoundly secret. There seems no doubt that we shall in the first instance go to Abrantes, but further all is lost in uncertainty. It will be several Days before our Division moves. Most unfortunately the weather has this Day assumed a very unpromising Appearance, and we much fear that the wet Season is about to set in.

11th. We still know nothing of our destination. It is considered very probable that we are going to the North of Portugal, as information has been received of the complete defeat of the Duke del Parque, and there is consequently no obstacle there to an irruption of the Army under Marshall Ney. The weather continues threatening, but the wet has not yet commenced.

16th. We are still without our Route, though it is hourly expected. At present our destination is Leyria. It is not unlikely however it may [be] changed on the March. We have had some heavy Rains and anticipate much more. The Sick were most of them sent from hence this Morning. Many are of opinion that we are about to embark: the Spaniards and Portugueze have no other idea. We are now a long time without News from England, which might probably throw some light on our future Operations. Indeed it is said that till Lord Wellington receives his next dispatches he is himself ignorant as to our remaining or otherwise in the country.

While writing the above the Route arrived. We march to-morrow morning for Abrantes, at which place we are to arrive on the 25th Inst. or Christmas Day. It is supposed on our arrival at Abrantes that we shall receive a further route.

17th. At twelve o'clock this day we bade adieu to Olivenza, and reached our resting place, Jerumenha, about three. It is a small village prettily situated on a high Hill, but affording very bad accommodation. Soon after our commencing our March the Rain set in, and we arrived at our Billets well drenched. Jerumenha is remarkable for having stood a long Siege under Marshall Schomberg, and again in the last War between the Spaniards and Portugueze. Distant from Olivenza two Leagues.

18th. Our march to-day was to Villa Vicosa about three Leagues or twelve Miles. We were again considerably annoyed by the wet. Villa Vicosa is one of the cleanest and neatest Towns in Portugal. It is a Royal Residence, and has attached to it a very extensive Park well stocked with Deer, where the Prince Regent was frequently accustomed formerly to hunt.

19th. We this day marched into Estremos, twelve miles from Villa Vicosa. This place I passed through on my way from Lisbon to Elvas, and was much pleased with its cleanliness over the other Towns I had observed in Portugal. The difficulty in procuring Billets was very great. The Juez de Foro or Chief Magistrate was a very good natured old man, but appeared to know very little of the Duty attached to his Situation. All the Billets he gave me proved of no use, and being at length apprehensive of getting no place for myself or Horses I remembered my good Friends at the Inn, who had treated me very well on my passing thro' this place before. On entering the House I was immediately recognised by all the Daughters, four in number, and received with a most hearty welcome, accompanied with the warmest Congratulations on my having quitted Spain in safety, a circumstance in the opinion of a Portugueze highly worthy of thanksgiving.

20th. We halted this Day at Estremos. In the course of the Day newspapers to the 29th Ulto. arrived. They state ten thousand men being about to embark for this Country,which has been confirmed by Letters received by different Officers. This renders it probable that the defence of this Country is certainly to be attempted.

21st. This Morning I bade adieu to my fair Hostesses at Estremos, who gave me their best wishes for my future welfare and assurance of the best reception if I should ever again travel this Road. I had been two Days and Nights in this Inn during which time I had a Fire constantly in my Room. They provided me with an excellent Bed and good Breakfasts, also Beds for my Servants and Stabling for my Horses. On going away I demanded my Bill and to my Astonishment found all the above comforts were provided for the moderate charge of four shillings and sixpence sterling.

Our march this day was to a miserable place called Cano, twelve Miles from Estremos. The Inhabitants are all poor, and the place furnishes nothing worthy of observation, excepting the extreme beauty with which the Olive Groves in the Neighbourhood are laid out.

22d. I was this Day detained at Cano several hours after the Regiment in procuring a Car for the conveyance of some Sick ; the Juez de Foro not being able to write or read was obliged to issue his orders verbally, which appeared to me to be very little regarded, and in consequence a considerable delay took place. While the old Gentleman was busy searching for the Car, I amused myself in conversing with his Daughter, a really pretty Girl, but as ignorant of everything not actually passing under her observation as a young savage in the wilds of America. She overwhelmed me with Questions as to the Modes and Customs of the English, and was particularly inquisitive as to the Ceremony of Matrimony. She had been taught to believe that an Englishman was by no means limited in the number of his Wives.

The Regiment halted this day at Avis, a dirty town, but well known for the Richness of its Convent. We were all quartered in this Building, which is certainly superior to anything of the kind I have before witnessed. The Rooms of the Friars, instead of being Cells (as they are generally termed), are extremely well furnished, and have an elegance and neatness about them scarcely observable in the private Houses of the richest Inhabitants. Notwithstanding these People plead poverty.

Here we learned that on our arrival at Abrantes we should receive a further Route to Coimbra, a distance of about ninety miles.

24th. We did not quit Avis till this morning, and our resting place to-night is at Ponte del Sor, a miserable Village affording nothing worthy of observation.

27th. We reached Abrantes on the 25th, and halted there that and the succeeding Day. It is a populous town, standing extremely high and capable of being very strongly fortified. Like most other Towns in this Country it is intolerably filthy, and on walking thro' it I felt much pleased that we were not to remain there. The Dukedom was bestowed by Buonapartè upon Junot, in consequence of its possessing some rich domains, and I have no doubt His Grace on his return here will make up his long Arrears with considerable interest. The Tagus runs at the bottom of the Hill on which the town stands. We crossed it by a Bridge of Boats, which might be almost instantly destroyed in case of necessity.

Our march this Day was to a small Village called Puenhete, standing also on the Banks of the River. The Day being beautiful and the Prospects fairer than anything I had before seen in Portugal rendered this Morning's travelling extremely pleasant. After our arrival here, having taken some refreshment, I ascended to a great eminence for the purpose of seeing a Convent, which however contained nothing remarkable. The scenery however from this height was finer than anything I ever saw, and were I compelled to live in Portugal I should doubtless choose this Situation ; the extent of view from it is immense ; on every side were to be seen extensive Olive Groves, and on the slopes of the Hills near the Tagus a variety of neat houses were interspersed. The serpentine course of the River in this neighbourhood adds much to the beauty of the Prospect. I was much fascinated with this scene, and I wished ardently for the power my sweet friend, C. M., possesses with her Pencil, that I might have taken a sketch of it.

30th. On the 28th we quitted Puenhete, and marched to Thomar, a considerable Town and Head-Quarters for the Portugueze Troops. Marshal Beresford is at present there. We had an opportunity of seeing one of the Regiments at Parade which have been drilled by English Officers. They were well clothed and made an excellent appearance. The Soldier-like Manner in which they went through their Evolutions astonished the English Officers. I should really expect much from them if opposed to the Enemy.

Our Commanding Officer was informed by Genl. Beresford that our march would not terminate at Coimbra. Guarda a town near the Frontiers is said to be our destination. The last week has been remarkably fine, which at this time of the Year we may consider a piece of singular good fortune.

Yesterday we halted at a small village called Aldeacruz, but affording an excellent Market and at a much cheaper rate than any other place we had been at in Portugal. We reached our present halting place (Leyria) this Afternoon where we are to remain to-morrow. Our Route this Day lay through a variety of Fir Groves, which for their extent and beauty are said to be unequalled.

Jan. 6th. We remained at Leyria on the 31st. The Town is old, and affords little worthy of note. On an Eminence near it stands a Ruin, which has long been considered as extremely fine. It was formerly a Moorish Castle of great strength. The Chapel still remains entire, but has not been used as a place of worship for some time. When the French were at Leyria, some Monks made resistance, and three of them were shot in the Chapel.

On New Year's Day we quitted Leyria, and marched to Pombal, a small Town, but known in History as having given a title to the most Eminent Minister that Portugal ever possessed. In a Convent there we saw a Coffin containing the remains of the celebrated Marquis, which, I know not for what reason, have never been interred. In the same Chapel was pointed out to us by the Friar who conducted us an Image of the Virgin, which he said had been put into a Fire of great heat but could not be consumed. The Image was of common Wood. Near it was a Record of various Miracles which had been performed thro' her intercession. We did not appear to doubt his Narratives, and I fancy he quitted us laughing up his sleeve at our apparent folly.

On the 2d. we marched to a small place called Condixe, which afforded a good Market and better accommodation than the exterior appearance of the Houses at first led us to expect. I do not know that the People as we go Northward are poorer than those of the South, but Shoes and Stockings are not to be seen amongst the lower Orders of Females since we quitted Leyria. The Men go well shod, with Stockings.

On the 3d. we reached Coimbra, the largest City in Portugal, with the exception of Lisbon and Oporto. It is the only University in the Kingdom, and appears to be at present thronged with Students. They are formed into a Corps, and many amongst them formerly distinguished themselves against the Enemy. These are distinguished by a Medal and Ribband. The common dress of the Students is a black Gown of Cloth over their common Dress, which is also all black. The Cap is likewise sable, and similar in shape to a double Night Cap.

This Town affords a great deal worthy of the attention of a Traveller. The Colleges, Convents, &c. &c. are very fine. There is also a Museum here which is said to contain a very

[1810]
[Jan.] rare collection of Natural Curiosities. Unfortunately my Time
there was so fully occupied by Duty that I was not able to
visit any of the Curiosities. My Billet there was excellent,
and my Bed·had so inviting an appearance, that I half feared
getting into it from an anticipation of the contrast I should
experience before reaching the end of my Journey. Here we
were made acquainted with our destination, which is a small
Town eighteen leagues from here called Celorico. The whole
Army are to be in Cantonments, at such distances as to be
easily brought together in case of necessity. It would appear
that Lord Wellington has no immediate expectation of a Visit
from the Enemy, as he purposes going to Lisbon, as the Army
are settled in their new Quarters. The Morning we quitted
Coimbra I saw him in his full dress uniform as Captain
General of Portugal, accompanied by Marshal Beresford and
a numerous Staff, going to review some Portugueze Regiments
The inhabitants were running out in crowds in [order] to see him;
indeed he is perfectly idolized by the Portugueze nation. On
this day he purposed quitting Coimbra for Viseu which is to
be Head-Quarters. I am informed by an Officer who dined
with him at Coimbra, that he never saw him in such spirits.
He has however at present a most serious responsibility upon
him.

Yesterday we had a most fatiguing march of nearly Thirty
Miles thro' infamous Roads. It was dark before we reached
our halting place, a miserable Village called Puente de
Murcella, affording the most wretched Accommodation. My
fears at Coimbra were here amply realised. We quitted the
place at eight o'clock this Morning, and reached our halting
place, Leyroza, at three in the Afternoon. It is almost deserted
by the former Inhabitants, but we are much better off than
last Night. The Scenery from Coimbra to this place is truly grand,
and quite exceeds an adequate description of it. The Hills are
immensely high, and the tops of the highest of them are
covered with Snow. Below all has the appearance of Spring,
from the extreme fineness of the weather, & from the

immense quantity of wood about here, which is all of the evergreen Species.

12th. On the 7th the Regiment marched for Penascos, but the Cars with the Convalescents not having come up I remained behind for them. It was late in the Afternoon before they arrived, when I proceeded with them to another Village about half a league in advance called Gallicis. Here we halted for the Night, and a most uncomfortable Evening I passed. My Room was exposed to all the keenness of a North wind which blew with uncommon violence. I could not procure a spark of Fire, and not having an individual to speak to made the Evening appear still more cheerless. Early the following morning we set out for Penascos, a distance of four long leagues thro' a wretched Road. On arriving there I found that the original Route of the Regiment was at present changed, and that instead of going to Celerico they had proceeded to Melo, a smaller place about three Leagues from hence & the same distance from Celerico. My Evening at Penascos was spent somewhat more pleasantly than the former one, the Night being finer and my Room less exposed. I passed a couple of Hours in the perusal of a French Poem I procured at Coimbra, called Pitié, from the pen of De Lille. It does equal Credit to the Head and Heart of its Author.

I forgot to state a circumstance which came under my observation at Leyrosa. It was Sunday, and when the Priest had finished the last Mass he repaired with several of the principal Inhabitants to the House of one of them. A Table being prepared for the purpose, and a Pack of Cards produced, they commenced gambling with an eagerness and avidity I scarcely ever before witnessed.

On the 9th I proceeded to this place, (Melo), and joined my Regiment, where we still remain. It is conjectured that we shall not march from here till the whole of the Troops going forward shall have passed through Celerico, which will not be before the 15th Inst.

Majr. A. (with whom I have messed during the whole of the March) is in the House of the Bishop of Guarda, who frequently resides here. He is a man of the most dignified deportment and of a truly liberal Mind. He supplies us with the most sumptuous Breakfasts and Dinners, and insists that we shall not procure a single Article as long as we remain in this place. The House may more properly be called his Nephew's, who is a Colonel in the Portugueze Service. The Dinners are cooked by the Wife of the latter, who evinces the utmost anxiety lest they should not be dressed according to our liking. The Bishop's chief Servant lived a great many years with an English Merchant in Lisbon, by which means he is of infinite use in directing the good Lady how to serve up a dinner a la Mode Anglaise.

Jan. 16. As there was yesterday no probability of our soon quitting this place, and our good Friend the Bishop still insisted upon supplying our Table, I determined, notwithstanding the kind manner in which he pressed me to continue, to secede from his House, and eat my Mutton Chop in my own Quarters, which resolution I accordingly put into execution. An Order however is just arrived for us to be in readiness to march at a Moment's Notice, and it is hinted we shall proceed to our original destination (Celerico) the Day after to-morrow. This place is about two hundred and fifty miles from Olivenza, and Celerico is about twelve Miles from hence. The Weather during our March was with the exception of one Day extremely fine. Since our arrival here it has almost constantly rained. To-day however it has cleared up, and promises to be fine. We may therefore be considered as extremely fortunate. The Enemy are advancing ; their Out Posts and our own are now very near each other. We may daily expect to hear of skirmishing, which must soon be followed by a general Engagement. The late Move of the Army has contributed very much to decrease the Sickness that so generally prevailed in it before.

20th. On the 18th we marched from Melo to Celerico. On our arrival there were surprised to find our Route still further extended to Guarda, one day's march in advance of Celerico, where we remain and are likely to remain, for some time. Guarda is said to be the highest City in Europe. The ascent to it from Celerico commences about a League from hence, and is extremely steep. About half way up the Hill we found ourselves amongst snow, which, we observed, increased in depth as we advanced to the Summit. Here we were enveloped in it. The cold is intense, not less severe than in the Northern parts of England; notwithstanding the Inhabitants are not more provided against it within doors than if it did not exist. There is not a fireplace in any of the Houses with the exception of the Kitchen. The only means of guarding against the cold are the Pans containing Charcoal, and these are frequently not to be used without at the same time having the windows open, on account of the pernicious tendency they possess in producing Head Aches.

A day or two since a Party of our Dragoons observed about thirty French Cavalry skirmishing near the Frontier; they did not sufficiently approach each other to come to blows. The Main Body of the Army must remain inactive for some time yet, the severity of the weather precluding the possibility of undertaking any military operations.

28th. We received certain accounts yesterday that the French are not making any demonstration of an intention to advance, nor does it appear that they have lately received any reinforcements. A large Fleet of Transports with Troops passed Oporto for Lisbon on the 12th Inst. and must have reached the latter place ere this.

We are at present inundated with reports. It is said that there is an insurrection in the South of France, headed by Madame Buonoparté (that Lady having been divorced), and aided by Talleyrand and Massena, and that in consequence the French Army is retreating from Spain. This piece of intelligence comes from the Duque del Parque, but very little credit is attached to it. Another rumour states that the French in endeavouring to force the passes of the Sierra Morena have been completely defeated by the Army under General Blake. Certain it is that there is an unaccountable inactivity amongst the Enemy. The utmost energy at the same time prevails both with the Spaniards and Portugueze in the organising of new levies, manufacturing of Arms, and fortifying of Cities, Passes, &c., &c. Notwithstanding the immense shock they look forward to from the power of France being likely to be concentrated against them, they anticipate more confidently than ever an eventual Triumph; and I observe likewise that many English Officers, who a few weeks back gave up the cause as entirely lost, now entertain an opinion that they may ultimately succeed. For my own part I have a much more favourable sentiment of the issue than I had at the period of our quitting Olivenza.

Febry 2d. It is said that the French are advancing into Portugal by way of Badajos and Elvas, and that their advance has actually reached Merida. Should this account prove correct, we shall most probably be compelled to measure back our steps in order to protect the Capital. Lord Wellington left Head-Quarters a Day or two since to proceed in that direction. The last English Newspapers concur in stating that he is to go out to India with full power to settle, if possible, the unhappy differences at present prevailing there. He is so completely idolized by the Portuguese, that I am confident his removal from the chief Command in this Country will excite more despondency among them than the loss of a general engagement. We have accts. of three hundred men having embarked to join our Battalion; which will render us so completely effective, that, whether affairs are soon brought to a termination or not in this Country, there is no prospect of our returning to England, as we shall doubtless be employed on some other Service. In the present critical and unsettled state of affairs it is impossible to conjecture where we may next be sent to serve; the Mediterranean, India, or North

America, it may be, will prove our destination. For my own part, so that our expatriation does not exceed three or four years, I care little where we go. The Mediterranean would certainly be the most pleasant, and India the most profitable. With respect to America I should have no other satisfaction in going there, than in the hopes of witnessing the chastisement they so richly deserve for their perfidious treatment to Great Britain, and their unnatural connexion with France.

I this day complete my twenty eighth year. An event of this kind cannot fail to produce in any mind in the least tinctured with humility many mortifying reflections. In ruminating over the years that are for ever gone past, the best of us have abundant cause of self-abasement in the recollection—to use the words of the Poet—" Of times misspent and fair occasions gone for ever by." Happy are those, who having learnt at length justly to appreciate the value of time, not only form sincere resolutions of not hereafter misspending it, but conscientiously and fully fulfil those resolutions. For my own part I look back with painful regret on the many, many hours I have myself passed without improvement, and while I resolve from henceforth to value it with a warmth proportionate to its worth I fear lest each succeeding year should make my retrospect still more painful. I look however with resignation for the assistance promised from above, feeling as I do so strongly the imperfection of Human Nature that without the Divine Aid I should tremble to be a partaker of it.

12th. Affairs are again putting on a bad aspect. It is confirmed beyond all doubt that the Enemy have forced the Passes of the Sierra Morena and that Seville is in their possession. Three Regiments just arrived at Lisbon from England, together with the 87th, who were on Garrison Duty there, sailed at three hours' Notice to assist the Spaniards at Cadiz in the protection of that place, and also to prevent the Fleet from falling into the hands of the Enemy. In the meantime we learn that the French are assembling in great force in the Neighbourhood of Salamanca, obviously with the intention of attacking us. It is morally impossible that we can remain long in our present position, our right and left Flank being both open to the Enemy. Lord Wellington is at present at Lisbon, concerting, it is supposed, with the Regency means for the defence of the Capital. The King's Speech, received a few days ago, renders it plain that this Country is not to be abandoned without a struggle. From the very serious defeats the Spaniards have recently sustained it is impossible not to look forward with more of fear than hope. The iniquities of this People are certainly at their height, & I feel convinced that the Judgments of God are upon them; when the Cup of His wrath shall be poured out, our finite understandings leave us no means of knowing; it will be happy for those Countries who have been hitherto exempt from the horrors of War—among which England stands eminently blessed—if they will take warnings from the afflictions of others, and not provoke too far the long suffering of the Almighty. I have myself no more doubt that these People are at present visited for their Iniquities, than I have that the Jews were formerly for the same cause. It is certain however that they regard not their Calamities in this light; on the contrary in their own Eyes theirs are the only Countries where God may be said to be truly worshipped. During my several visits to Catholic Kingdoms I have constantly observed the impression made on the Minds I have been most intimate with by the Religion they profess, and with a truth equal to the solemn occasion I can affirm I have never met with one whose heart appeared to be touched with a coal from the Holy Altar of God. As I have before observed, the Sabbath is wholly disregarded by them, or, if remembered, it is only as a Day when buying, selling, gaming, and other Amusements are pursued with more than common Avidity: indeed so completely is this Holy Day prostituted that I see no means left them but expunging from the Decalogue the fourth Commandment in the same manner they have long since done the second. For every species of wickedness the Town [where] I am writing is eminently perspicuous : Common decency while performing their most solemn Services is not to be observed ; the most disgusting levity, even while burying the Dead, is constantly practised—I mean by the Priests themselves. These Men in conversation allow themselves a latitude, or rather, licentiousness, only to be credited by those who have heard them. Even in a Convent of Nuns here, in a place and by a People solemnly devoted to the Service of God, Conversations daily take place between them and (I am ashamed to say,) certain British Officers, from which the most abandoned women in England would turn away with disgust. In this place Chastity in women is scarcely considered a virtue, and it is notorious that nine-tenths of the seductions are traced to the Clergy ; yet these men continue notwithstanding to possess an unbounded influence over the minds of the other Orders of the People ; and so they will continue to do, till by the inscrutable, but sure, operations of the Almighty a pure Religion is introduced among them, and the present system of Idolatry is for ever abolished. That the successes of the French are contributing to this great end I have no doubt, and contemplating the present extraordinary state of Affairs in a moral view, I look upon Buonapartè, notwithstanding his unworthiness, as an Instrument in the Hand of Providence for the completion of this great work. His antipathy to Convents and Monks is notorious, and as he extends his Conquests he goes on annihilating these Institutions regarding them, (as I do) in the light of Hotbeds of Iniquity. I consider this as no small step gained ; and as he likewise permits men to think for themselves in matters of Religion, from which they have been hitherto debarred, I think it may be reasonably expected that an emancipation from the Shackles in which they have so long been held is a circumstance likely to flow naturally from the change this freedom will introduce into Men's Minds. This subject has occupied me much within these few last days ; and it is under this view of it that I think it even desirable that the French should eventually succeed in subjugating Spain and Portugal.

13th The Enemy have made an advance of four Leagues. They are at present about two Leagues on the other side of Ciudad Rodrigo, with the intention, it is supposed, of making an attack on that place. The Inhabitants of Guarda are in the utmost state of Consternation. Lord Wellington's absence they consider as the greatest possible Misfortune that could happen at this juncture. His Name is with them quite a Host of itself. They know by sad experience what it is to be visited by the French. They were here for a few days, and during that time they laid the People under very heavy contributions: besides which their general Conduct was brutal and ferocious in the extreme.

21st. The Enemy advanced, as was supposed would be the case, upon Ciudad Rodrigo, and after throwing a few Shots & Shells into the place retired to their former Positions. This movement, it is suspected, was merely intended to keep us on the alert here, and prevent our making any Motions to impede whatever other objects they may have in view in other places. It appears certain that Badajos is invested, & that the French have possessed themselves of Olivenza. General Hill with his Division has marched from Abrantes, but whether to relieve Badajos or to cover the retreat of the Sick from Elvas is not known. From the Enemy pushing forward in so many different directions it is generally and naturally supposed they have received large Reinforcements. We hear they were admitted into Seville, not only without resistance, but with every apparent mark of Satisfaction. On mentioning this to a Portugueze, he exclaims "What can you expect from Spaniards?" In the mean time we are expecting here that these circumstances must soon lead to an evacuation of the Peninsula, tho' from the determined Character of Lord Wellington it is expected he will dispute every inch of the Ground. The Troops in general continue very healthy. What few Sick there are are sent weekly to Coimbra, in order that the Army may be left to act free and unincumbered. As a precautionary measure the whole of the heavy Baggage has been embarked at Lisbon.

The Weather continues excessively cold, and we are informed that the Snow and Frost prevail here till the middle of June. The Inhabitants say that the only tolerably fine time of the Year here is in the Months of August and September. Perhaps as a residence it is one of the most unpleasant Situations in Europe; its extreme height renders it very inconvenient for taking exercise on Horseback, and its extreme dirtiness makes it as unpleasant to take exercise on Foot.

[MARCH] March 3. Nothing particular has occurred within these few Days. The Enemy remains at Salamanca, and there is reason to believe they have not been reinforced. It is rumoured with some degree of confidence that they lost three thousand Men in an Attack upon Cadiz, but there are so many reports constantly going about that it is impossible to know what to believe. A few Evenings since there was some skirmishing between a small party of our Riflemen & about two hundred French. The latter left four dead; we had not a Man hurt.

11th. The Enemy continue occasionally to show themselves; but it does not appear that their main Body is in advance of Salamanca. It is stated that Junot has arrived there with thirty thousand men and that preparations are making for the reception of Buonapartè. The News of one Day is however generally falsified the next. We expect to know something decisive by the next Mail respecting our remaining in this Country. As long as a British Army is in Portugal, the People have no apprehension of danger; but they say, if left to themselves, their doom at once is fixed.

This being the Season of Lent, there is abundance of Fasting and Praying, but as little Devotion as at other Times. The three Days prior to Ash Wednesday there was some very beautiful Music and singing in the Cathedral; the Organ is a remarkably good one, and one of the Priests possesses the finest Bass Voice I ever heard. Processions and Ceremonies are numerous, and the consumption of wax Candles is immense. The number of Priests attached to the Cathedral alone is very great, a Bishop, a Dean, three others possessing high Rank, but difficult of pronunciation, thirty Canons, and a vast number of inferior Clergy. I was witness to the Ceremony of Matrimony a few days since. It has a strong resemblance to that of the Reformed Church, but the greatest levity prevailed during the whole Service. The Bride did not appear to be more than twelve or thirteen, and made her Responses with the utmost pertness. The Bridegroom had the appearance of a Person going to be involved in a different species of Noose from that of Matrimony.

17th. There is little doubt that the Enemy have received large reinforcements under Junôt. Slight Skirmishes continue occasionally to take place. The idea that we must almost immediately abandon our present Position is general, and we are in daily expectation of an order to that effect. It is the Opinion of every one that, immediately we begin our Retreat, the French will advance in this direction, and annoy us by every possible means. Indeed our distance from the place of Embarkation is so great, that it is to be feared before reaching it our Casualties will be very numerous.

The three hundred Men from England joined us a few days since, and a very fine detachment they certainly are. The 40th may with truth be considered at present the very finest Regiment in the Army. Our strength including Sergeants & Drummers is near thirteen hundred men. I feel the responsibility attached to the care of so large a body.

The weather is very bad ; the Rains are incessant, and come down in Torrents. Notwithstanding, the Army generally is in as good, if not better, Health than a Force of the same magnitude would be in England. This being St. Patrick's Day I much fear lest the intemperance that will certainly prevail should be the cause of Disease to many. The Regimental Bands played through the Streets, as is usual on this occasion, commencing at Midnight. On hearing it the Inhabitants were elated with hope, conceiving it could be from no other reason than the arrival of some great News.

21st. The night before last at midnight fifteen hundred French, led on by a General Officer of four and twenty and a great favourite of Buonapartè, attacked four Companies of the Rifle Corps under the command of Colonel Beckwith. Notwithstanding the superiority of their numbers the French were completely defeated with great loss. The Rifle Corps had one Officer and three Men killed and six Men wounded. The Affair was a very brilliant one, and the Rifle Corps maintained by their gallant conduct that character for Valour which has so eminently and so long distinguished them.

The weather appears to have set in fine. Hostilities may therefore be expected almost immediately to commence on a larger scale.

27th. The Enemy have again retired to Salamanca, and there are Accounts, which rest on very good Authority, that reinforcements which had actually entered Spain have been suddenly ordered to return to France ; Marshal Ney has likewise been sent for express to Paris. These circumstances are said to have originated in consequence of a dispute between France and Russia, which is likely to terminate in a Rupture between the two Powers. The next Packet from England will inform us as to the truth or falsehood of this Rumour, which has certainly obtained much credit. We are now an unusual time without a Mail—so much so that Fears are entertained for the Safety of the Packet. We have had no London Papers since the 14th of last month.

Having described the ceremonies of Marriage and Burial in these Countries I am now enabled to add that of Baptism, having witnessed it a few days since in the Cathedral in this

[1810]
[MARCH] place. The Sponsors are four in number, two of each sex. After a few Initiatory Prayers, some salt previously consecrated is stuffed into the Child's Mouth; after which the Priest inserts Saliva from his own Mouth into the Ears and Nostrils of the Baptised; a variety of other ceremonies being gone through, the unfortunate Infant is stripped perfectly naked and immersed in the coldest water; a few more Prayers conclude the ceremony. This I saw practised on a Child of three days old. The same laughing & other marks of irreverence prevailed during this Ceremony as at the others I have before noticed.

31st. The long expected Packet has at length arrived and with it Papers to the 15th Inst. They do not confirm the intelligence so confidently reported of Russia having declared War against France, nor indeed do they mention anything that can lead to the probability of such an event. His Majesty's message for taking thirty thousand Portugueze into British Pay having been approved by both Houses of Parliament renders it no longer doubtful that the utmost is to be done for the preservation of this Country. This decision is a source of considerable disappointment to many individuals in this Army. For my own part, tho' I see no prospect of ultimately retaining our ground here, yet I do not think we can abandon these People without a struggle without sacrificing the National Character. We may probably sustain much loss, but even that I consider as not to be estimated when the Honour of England is at stake.

The weather is excessively gloomy, and remarkably cold when the Latitude of this place is considered. The Climate of England I consider much less variable than that of this part of Portugal.

[APRIL] April 6th. This afternoon three soldiers of the 27th Regiment were executed in the presence of the whole Garrison. They were convicted of Housebreaking, a Crime Lord Wellington has declared he will never pardon. They were all very young, and met their Fate with great firmness. The scene was truly melancholy, and was, I think, calculated to generate any other sentiment than that of Pride in the Hearts of the Spectators. For my own part I felt that I could not exclaim with the Pharisee—" I thank Thee, O God, that I am not as these Men, &c." The predominating sentiment in my Breast was Humility together with a pious Gratitude to that Being who had blessed me with Parents whose united Precept and Example had taught me in early life to distinguish right from wrong. The Execution was performed in as heavy a Snow Storm as I ever experienced.

Several fresh Regiments have, it seems, arrived at Lisbon from England, which must convince the most sceptical that every effort is to be made to preserve this Country. We hear that an Ambassador has arrived in London from Paris, but no one appears to think that Peace can possibly be the Consequence. For my own part I see not how such an Event can anyhow be treated for, as long as we retain a footing in the Peninsula. Were the French absolute Masters of Spain and Portugal the case would be widely different.

April 9th. I was yesterday attracted into the Cathedral by seeing an unusual Number of Persons entering it, and on enquiry found it was Passion Sunday, tho' with us Palm Sunday. The sermon treated on the Sufferings and Death of our Saviour, and was delivered in a tone of voice bordering on crying; this I was afterwards informed the Preacher is obliged to do. During a particular part of the Discourse, and, while he is describing in the most forcible language the extent of those Sufferings, a Curtain is suddenly drawn back by an invisible Hand, and an Image of our Lord upon the Cross is exposed. The whole Female part of the Congregation immediately commence an audible lamentation, which from its generality I could not conceive to be real. The Sermon is soon after concluded, when the whole Congregation strike their Faces repeatedly with their Hands and dismiss.

13th. We are entirely without News of the Enemy in this Quarter. The weather appears likely to be more favourable than it has lately been, from which many infer we shall soon be engaged. Regiments continue to arrive from England at Lisbon, and indeed every circumstance tends to prove that there will yet be a most obstinate Struggle before the fate of this Country is finally fixed.

26th. Last week, being Passion Week, was one continual round of Ceremonies and Processions ; were I to attempt to describe them all this Book would be insufficient for the purpose. The Thursday is here a more solemn Day than the Friday, and every person who lays the smallest claim to the denomination of a good Catholic makes a point of confessing on that Day and afterwards communicating. I had an opportunity of being present at the different functions performed in the Chapel of the Nuns. The Organ is a very sweet one, and some of the Music particularly fine, but the levity I have so frequently observed among the Canons in the Cathedral may be styled Devotion in comparison with that which prevails among these fair Recluses. I never before had so convincing a proof of the inefficiency of this Religion to touch and amend the Heart.

May 10th. Since the last date the Enemy have made various movements indicating a disposition to attack us. Lord Wellington in consequence removed his Head Quarters to Celerico to be nearer the scene of action, and the whole British Force together with several Portugueze Regiments have been concentrated in this Neighbourhood. It is said however that the French have again retreated upon Salamanca, and that they may still be some time longer quiet. Notwithstanding the advanced Season of the Year the weather is cold and almost constantly wet, nor do the Inhabitants give us hopes of having better, at least for a Month to come. It is true we have not had any Snow very lately, but they bid us prepare to expect it.

By papers from England to the 20th Ulto. we have an account of the late disturbances in the Metropolis. I much fear that the flame is only partially smothered, to break out at some future Day with augmented violence. It is melancholy to reflect how the lower Orders of People are led away. Could they but compare their lot with those of other Countries, they would be sensible of the numerous Blessings and Privileges they enjoy. This clamour for reform is made by designing men a cloak for the most pernicious and iniquitous Intentions.

30th. We still remain here unmolested, though the Enemy have according to all Accts. been reinforced to an immense Number. This inaction on their part is attributed to the quantity of Water in the Rivers between them and us, which have been and still are greatly swollen by the constant and violent Rains that have lately prevailed.

On the verge of June we have not anything in this place that indicates the approach of Summer. A Fire is still as desirable as it is in England in the Month of May. By descending the Mountain however on which this City stands we can at once change our Temperature many degrees. Nothing can be more beautiful than is the Valley at the Foot of the Hill about four Miles from hence. So sensible are the natives of the superiority of this charming Spot that everyone of them who can scrape together a little money builds a Quintal or Cottage there; it is now extremely populous. A variety of sketches of this valley have been taken by different Draughtsmen. Indeed, on descending the Hill, it forms a Landscape equal, if not superior, in Beauty to anything I ever before witnessed.

I had a few Days since an Opportunity of going through the Convent in this place. I went in with a Staff Officer, who got admission under the pretext that it was necessary for him to take the altitudes of the surrounding Mountains from a high Tower belonging to the Convent, where the

Sisterhood go to take the Air. The Abbess was completely taken in, and two Confessors being at hand to accompany us we were accordingly admitted. On the Door being opened the Abbess attended by Twenty Nuns presented themselves to pay their respects. As soon as we thought we had been a reasonable time in measuring distances we proposed to descend, when one of the Nuns whispered us to ask permission to see the whole of the Convent, which the Abbess at once granted. So pleased were the Sisterhood with this Visit, (the first they had ever known), that there was not a Nook, Cranny, or Corner, they did not in a whisper suggest to us to ask the Abbess to be permitted to see. In the Chapel we were favoured with some Solos and Duets executed in very superior stile and accompanied by the Organ. Being a Medical Man I was allowed to visit their Infirmary, where I saw a Nun a hundred and five years old in the possession of all her Faculties except her Sight. Not knowing I was near her, she was expressing to the Nuns who accompanied me her Surprise and Indignation that anything like a Man should be permitted to enter the Convent. We at length took our leave. The Abbess, whose Heart appears to be better than her Head, has been since made to believe it was a trick, and I fancy she will not again open the Doors on such a pretext.

June 2d. Everything indicates an immediate movement. An Order has been issued for each Regiment to be prepared to march at half an hour's Notice; every Man not entirely fit for Service has been sent away, and one Day's Provisions are kept constantly cooked beforehand. Whether this Movement will be forward or backward, to the right or left, we are in profound ignorance. The Weather has become fine, and it does not appear probable that an Engagement between the two Armies can be many Days delayed.

23d. We still remain at Guarda, and our quitting it appears to depend entirely upon the Movements of the

Enemy. They are now actively besieging Ciudad Rodrigo, and, their Heavy Artillery having arrived, there is little probability of its holding out many Days. They are now in such force that it is generally conceived they will immediately after advance into this Country, & almost everyone appears to think that we cannot make any effectual resistance to their progress. Our advanced Picquets are constantly in sight of those of the Enemy, and the Men frequently approach so near to each other as to hold Conversations. They say it is nothing less than madness our remaining here, and that if we do not speedily fly to our Ships we shall inevitably all be eat up.

25th. Head Quarters remove this day to Almeida, but there are no Orders as yet for the Troops to accompany them. The Army is at present so generally healthy, that it is supposed Lord Wellington will defer hutting them as long as possible.—Almeida is distant from the French Head Quarters only six Leagues.

Yesterday commenced here a large Fair, notwithstanding its being Sunday, thus furnishing another instance of the total disregard paid to the Divine Ordinances by a People assuming to themselves an extraordinary degree of Religion, and excluding from the Ark of God's Mercy all those whose Religion tends to differ from theirs.

[JULY] July 10th. Ciudad Rodrigo still holds out, and furnishes another instance of the extraordinary valour with which the Spaniards defend their Cities. The Enemy have three times attempted to storm the place with chosen Troops, and each time have been repulsed with great slaughter. The defence of the Garrison has excited universal admiration. The weather is extremely fine, and at this time of the year Guarda may be considered a very pleasant Quarter, as from its height there is an almost constant breeze : in the Valleys the heat is excessive, and the Troops are less healthy than those here.

The Marquis Romana passed thro' here a few Days since on his return to Badajos.   He had been to Head Quarters to have an interview with Lord Wellington.   He speaks, I am told, with great confidence of the ultimate triumph of Spain over her oppressors.   He is most devoted to his Country, and I really believe determined not to survive the extinction of her liberty.   His appearance proves that a very great soul does sometimes inhabit a very mean body.

12th.   The enemy entered Ciudad Rodrigo by Capitulation the Evening before last.   Conjecture is afloat as to what will be their next movement.   Some think they will push on for Almeida; others are of opinion they will direct their force against Badajos.   A short time will determine.

In a skirmish Yesterday Colonel Talbot of the 14th Dragoons was killed.   He is much lamented.

The Night before last a most horrid Murder was committed a short distance from this place.   There is too much reason to suppose that the perpetrators were British. I was directed by the General Yesterday Morning to go down there, when the most dreadful Sight I ever witnessed presented itself.   Three Bodies, viz., a Man, Woman, and their Daughter, a Child about eight years of Age, lay on the Floor, weltering in Blood; the former and the latter quite dead, and the Mother with little sign of Life.   A Hatchet lay beside them with which the deed had evidently been completed.   The Heads of the deceased were literally beat to a Jelly.   The Woman still lives, and there are hopes of her recovery.   She is at present incapable of making a deposition, but her return to reason is anxiously looked for, in the hope that it may lead to the discovery of the Murderers.   The wretches were doubtless instigated to the Murder from the fear of discovery, as Lord Wellington invariably punishes Housebreaking with death.

21st. The enemy continue in force about Ciudad Rodrigo, and there is every reason to suppose they will immediately commence the Siege of Almeida. Genl. Loison, equally notorious for his infamy & his impudence, sent in a few days since a message to Lord Wellington offering him a bet of five hundred Guineas that he would not dare to attempt to raise the Siege of Almeida whenever it should be attacked. Lord W's intentions as far as regards that Fortress are profoundly secret. It is very strong and well provisioned; consequently a protracted defence is expected from it.

25th. Affairs are evidently drawing to a Crisis. The Light Brigade had yesterday a very severe action in attempting to defend a Bridge over the Coa. By the great superiority of the Enemy they were repulsed on the third attack with the loss of twenty-two Officers killed & wounded; our loss in Men has not yet transpired. Several Regiments that formed the advance are expected in here this Afternoon. As the Garrison here has no order to march, many are of opinion that a stand is to be made in this place.

26th. It appears that the Enemy did not succeed in forcing the Bridge, but they were themselves compelled to retire. Genl. Crawford remained in possession for several hours, but thought it prudent to retire in the Evening. Our loss amounted to thirty Officers and six hundred & fifty men. The loss to the French is not known, but it must have been very great. Their force was more than two to one.

There has been a great deal of firing the whole of this Day from the Batteries at Almeida, from which it is conjectured that the Enemy are raising Works in order to commence the Siege of that Fortress.

The People here are in the greatest possible consternation; Cars and Mules laden with valuables are hourly leaving the Town, and I apprehend the greater number of Inhabitants will quit the place on the near approach of the French.

30th. We now form the advance of the Army, and there is no doubt shall commence our retreat, as soon as the Enemy show themselves in force, it being generally believed that Lord Wellington has at present no intention of bringing the French to an Engagement. This place is nearly deserted, scarcely a family remaining. The Nuns have quitted the Convent, having obtained a Dispensation for that purpose. With the exception of two or three they left it almost broken hearted. I was particularly affected at seeing one of them (the oldest of the community and who I find is one hundred and seventeen years of age) quit the place she had not been out of before for seventy-six years. She has kept her Bed a great while, but with the exception of her Sight she retains all her faculties. She was laid on a Car, and bore her Sufferings without a Murmur, but fervently praying that she might be released from them while on the Road to the place she was going to. Having been in the building every Day the last six weeks attending on a sick Nun, I had an opportunity of knowing several of them, and most worthy People many of them were, particularly the Lady Abbess. She quitted the Convent last night, and I attended her some distance out of the Town. She evidently laboured under the severest mental Anguish : my Heart bled for her. On parting with her she offered up a most fervent Prayer for my happiness here and hereafter, and assured me that it would afford her the most sincere gratification, could I in the event of getting safe out of the Country find means to make her acquainted with it.

We perceive distinctly the Firing at Almeida, which is to-day carried on on both sides with great spirit. Our Baggage is kept constantly packed, but we do not expect to march till the Enemy shall have possessed themselves of that Garrison.

[1810]
[August]

Augst. 4th. The Enemy continue before Almeida, but, as all communication is cut off between that place and this, we are ignorant of the progress they make in the Siege. They pushed their Patrols last night within a league and a half of this Garrison. Lord Wellington is at Celerico, but the main body of the Army is considerably in the rear. It is now generally conceived that Lord W. will, if possible, bring the Enemy to action between Ponte de Murcella & Coimbra, and from the very great strength of the Position he augurs a complete triumph.

6th. This Morning pursuant to the sentence of a general Court Martial two soldiers of the 97th Regiment were shot in presence of the whole Garrison paraded for that purpose. The one was a German, the other an Irishman. They met their fate with remarkable firmness.

A large party of Portugueze Peasantry yesterday attacked a French foraging Party, & succeeded in killing an officer and twenty-four men. They came in here this Morning, bringing with them the Horses & Arms of the Enemy. From the enormities committed by the French, it is not to be wondered at that the Portugueze pursue so sanguinary a mode of warfare; but, if persisted in, the war must inevitably become a war of extermination.

9th. The Enemy have not yet opened their Batteries on Almeida. It is difficult to account for this delay. The Deserters and Prisoners generally agree that they will not advance into this Country till the Conquest of that Fortress shall have been effected. In the meantime Lord W. is making every preparation to give them a warm reception. We amuse ourselves in this place chiefly at Cricket, and from the ground where we play can distinctly see the Fire from the Garrison of Almeida. From the Spirit with which the Officers in general enter into this game one would hardly suppose there was an Enemy within an hundred Leagues of us.

A Spaniard well-known by the Name of Don Julian was here yesterday on his way to Celerico to have an interview with Lord Wellington. He is a most enterprising Character, and in the last three Months has succeeded in destroying a great Number of the Enemy. He gives no Quarter to any who make resistance. His followers sometimes amount to a thousand, at others he cannot muster fifty. They make a great deal by plunder, and absent themselves for the purpose of spending their Money ; which having done they again join his Standard.

19th. The Enemy have only this Day opened their Batteries. The Firing on both Sides has been terrible. Various are the Opinions as to the time the Garrison will be able to hold out, a Week, ten Days, a Month, and some think even to the first of October. Every Day will be of consequence as the Harvest is nearly all in, and there will be time afforded to transport it to the Rear, which must greatly distress the Enemy when they advance.

21st. Head Quarters remove this Day to Alverche, and the Regts. in the rear are marching forward. Whether it is intended to relieve Almeida or not must soon be determined. This Movement has excited much confidence among the People here.

31st. Since the last date affairs have very materially altered. It appears the Enemy did not open upon Almeida till the 26th, and not on the 19th as was supposed. That same Evening a Shell fell into a large Building containing the Powder and Ammunition in an immense quantity, which exploded and destroyed the whole Town. The loss of lives on this melancholy occasion amounted it is said to upwards of a thousand. The Garrison capitulated on the 28th in consequence of this unlucky and unforeseen event. Measures of the utmost precaution have been adopted by Lord Wellington. The whole Army was Yesterday Morning in

Motion ; the Brigade of General Campbell in the Valley of Mondego moved a day's march towards Coimbra, and Genl. Cole's Brigade, in which is the 40th, moved to the Valley. A Battalion of Light Infantry alone remains in Guarda. The Town itself is almost entirely forsaken by the Inhabitants. None but the poorest Class of Inhabitants remain. We are quartered in a Village called Faya situated on the Mondego. Our sojourn here of course depends on the Movements of the Enemy. The Valley is certainly one of the most beautiful situations in Portugal. The Vines are in immense abundance ; but the Grapes will not be ripe this Fortnight, and ere that in all probability we shall have retrograded many Leagues.

It does not appear that any blame attaches to Col. Cox, the Governor of Almeida. The powder was secured in a Bomb Proof, and it is supposed a train must have been unfortunately laid from some damaged Bag, on which a Shell fell and caused the fatal explosion. Col. C. did not surrender till he had fired away the last round of Ammunition. He was much beloved by the Garrison. He is of course (with the few other English Officers that were at Almeida) a prisoner of war.

[SEPT.] Sepr. 5th. On the 2d. instant we received orders to quit Faya, and proceeded to a village called Villa de Porco, half a League distant only, but more in the line of March in case of a sudden Order. We had just begun to make ourselves comfortable in this latter place, when we were directed to proceed as quick as possible to Lenhares, intelligence having been received that the Enemy had forced our Dragoons at Alverca, and that they were only two Leagues and a half from us on our Flank. It was nearly dark when we marched. Our road lay across the Mountains through a Road nearly impassable. The night being dark rendered the March a most fatiguing one. It was nearly four in the Morning when we reached Lenhares, pretty well tired. On our arrival there we found an order to proceed again at five for a village called Santa Marinha. The Day being very hot, the Men were generally quite knocked up by the time they reached their Quarters. Santa Marinha is a large but extremely irregular Village situated in a beautiful Country, half a League out of the Road from Celerico to Coimbra. We fully expected to have marched again Yesterday Morning, but the French do not appear to be advancing. Our Dragoons patrolled yesterday into Guarda, but could see nothing of them. General Cotton with the Cavalry is at Celerico, five leagues in our rear. Lord Wellington is at a place called Gouvea about a League from hence. Between our Division and the Dragoons is the Light Division under Genl. Crawford ; the remaining part of the Army is in our front.

7th. I rode this morning to Head Quarters, but was not able to collect a particle of News. The general opinion there is that the Contest in this Country is likely to be a very protracted one. The Enemy show no disposition whatever to advance. Our Picquets remain in Guarda ; at Gouvea is a very large Convent, formally a celebrated retreat of the Jesuits but latterly inhabited by Nuns ; they however with the other Societies of that kind have quitted their retirement and fled to their Friends.

11th. Intelligence has reached Head Quarters that the French entered Guarda on the evening of the 9th, and that Massena was to have his Head Quarters at Pinhel as yesterday. From the exhausted state of that part of the Country it is generally conceived they cannot remain there, but must either advance upon us or otherwise make a retrogade movement. With all our Money and the Comman of the Country the Commissariat have great difficulty in supplying the Army. Unfortunately the Indian Corn is not yet ripe, or we should not leave the Enemy a single Article of subsistence.

17th. At nine in the Evening of the 15th we received Orders to march the following Morning at Day Break. This order was supposed to be in consequence of the Enemy having entered the Valley of Mondego. Our Route was to a small village called Vigea : at that place we had scarcely begun to make ourselves comfortable, when another order arrived to proceed without delay to Gallicis, two Leagues further on the road towards Ponte de Murcella. It was dark before we reached it. We continued our March this Morning, and after a great deal of Order, Counter Order and Disorder reached this place (Villa Cova) about Noon. It is the same distance from Ponte de Murcella as the place we remained at last Night, *viz.*, five Leagues. Whatever are the present Movements of the Enemy, the Army is kept in entire ignorance of them ; but from the short time we are now allowed to halt we conclude they are advancing upon us.

19th. At Daylight Yesterday Morng. we quitted Villa Cova, and after a long march through a Country more abounding in beautiful Scenery than Corn or Wine halted for the Night at a small Village called Paradella. This Morning we resumed our Route, and passed the Puente de Murcella, where our grand stand was to have been made. Our halt for the Night is at a Village called San Miguel, about a mile out of the high Road to Coimbra, and four Leagues from that City. The Enemy, it is supposed, aware of the immense strength of the position about Puente de Murcella have declined taking this route, and are gone by Vizeu. If they hope to reach Coimbra before us they will be mistaken, as two Divisions of the British Army enter it this Evening. The Country round Coimbra is extremely strong and capable of defence. Many are therefore of opinion that Lord Wellington will make a stand there. Others think we shall not oppose the enemy till we reach Leyria, which is a still stronger Position. There is every reason to believe that the French Army is by no means so strong as has been supposed.

Indeed it is now confidently asserted that they cannot bring sixty thousand musquets into the Field, and, as they advance into the interior, their force will rapidly decrease from Sickness and other Casualties. On the contrary we are retreating upon reinforcements. Besides a considerable force landed a few days since in Lisbon, accounts have this day reached Head Quarters of the arrival of three thousand men in Mondego Bay, which from their proximity can immediately join the Army. Certain it is that we never anticipated with so much confidence as at present the entire defeat of the Enemy, should they dare to attack us.

22d. On the 20th at daylight we quitted San Miguel, and in the course of the forenoon crossed the Mondego at a Ford called Barca de Conselto. The crossing of the River excited a good deal of astonishment throughout the Army, as it was generally supposed that our Position would be immediately in the vicinity of Coimbra. Our halt that night was at Penna Cova, where we found very good accommodation, and from the circumstance of our advancing towards the Enemy the Inhabitants were more civil than we had experienced from them while we were retrograding. Yesterday Morning we again commenced our route and marched several Leagues thro' cross Roads, till we reached the high Road leading from Coimbra to Vizeu. We halted at a most miserable Village called Sula, where we could with difficulty procure covering even for the Officers, the Men being obliged to go into Huts. Here we still remain, and are likely to do so till the Enemy come on us, our positions being all round this Neighbourhood. Nothing in appearance can be stronger than the Country about here. The Roads are extremely narrow, passing through immense Chains of Mountains, which will entirely prevent the Cavalry of the Enemy from getting into Action. Our advanced Parties are continually skirmishing. The Portugueze under Brigr. Genl. Pack were yesterday engaged, and very much distinguished themselves.

They took fifty Prisoners. The French as they advance use the Inhabitants most cruelly, from which we infer that they despair themselves of gaining the Country, or otherwise they would be more likely to conciliate. Lord Wellington's Head Quarters are near this place, at a celebrated Convent called Busaco. It is the finest building of the kind in Portugal, and well known formerly as an Exile for Persons of Rank from the Court. Lord W. is constantly on Horseback reconnoitring, and if we may judge from his Countenance & Spirits he anticipates a complete triumph over the Enemy. This place is about four Leagues from Coimbra, and the Advanced Posts of the French are within two Leagues of us.

24th. We still remain at Sula, but are in constant expectation of an order to change our ground a little more to the left. There was smart skirmishing yesterday a few miles in our front. The firing was very loud and distinct. Last night the whole of the Cavalry retired to our rear. The Light Division continue in advance. If hardly pressed they will fall back upon us, and the action is then likely to become general. All has been quiet hitherto this Day, and it is now past Noon.

[Ocт.] October 7th. I take up my Narrative from the last Date, which has been a most eventful period, but, having lost my Memorandums, my sketch will, I fear, be very imperfect. On the 25th Ulto. the attack of the Enemy on our Light Troops was of that Nature, that the Comr. of the Forces, perceiving they meditated a general attack, directed them to retire, which they did in the most perfect order. In the meantime the whole Army took up its position on a ridge of Mountains a little way in the rear of the Villages they had occupied. This position may justly be considered one of the strongest in the World. The enemy advanced to the ground we had quitted. Hope brightened the countenance of Lord Wellington, as he observed their approach. Skirmishing continued during the Afternoon, but nothing material occurred. On the morning of the 26th there was a thick Fog, which at length cleared up, and displayed to each other the Rival Armies drawn up on opposite Hills. A Valley between of considerable breadth separated them : their Numbers appeared most formidable, but the eagerness evinced by our Troops to receive their attack may have been equalled but can never have been surpassed. The Morning passed with only now and then a random Shot. They were evidently unprepared. In the afternoon the skirmishing between the Light Troops became brisk ; it ceased at Dusk without much loss on either side. General Officers were observed busily reconnoitring our Position, and the expectation of an Attack the following Morning was universal.—Our ideas were well founded ; at dawn of Day the Enemy made a most furious Assault upon our Right & Centre. All remained quiet on the left, in which was our Division. We were consequently Spectators, and a most gratifying view we had of the whole Affair. Lord W. had directed the Troops to suffer the Enemy to come within a short distance of the top of the Hill, when they were to give them a deliberate Volley and charge. This we distinctly observed. They were almost instantly thrown into the greatest confusion, and fled precipitately. This Action lasted but a short time, and skirmishing concluded the Day. It was a subject of universal regret that they did not make a general attack upon us. From the nature of our position, and the valour of our Troops, there is little doubt but their Army would have been nearly annihilated. Our loss this day was, including Portugueze, seven hundred in killed and wounded. That of the enemy, as we have since been able pretty correctly to ascertain, was six General Officers, a great number of other Officers, and four thousand Men. Gratifying as was the result of this Battle it was more particularly so from the great gallantry evinced by our Allies the Portugueze. It was true much had been expected from them by many, but there was a possibility of their failing in the hour of trial. Such however was their conduct during the Action (and they were very much engaged) that they gained the entire admiration of the whole British Army. Indeed they performed several individual Acts of Heroism that would have done honour to the Veteran Troops of any Nation. Having failed in their attempts on our right and centre, we were in hopes they would the next morning (28th) endeavour to force our left. In this however we were deceived. All remained tranquil, with the exception of skirmishing between the Sharp Shooters. They did not appear so numerous this Day as before, and in the afternoon we observed their Cavalry in motion & moving to the Rear. The opinion now became general, that they would no more attempt to dislodge us, but that they would either retrace their steps to the Frontiers, or otherwise endeavour to turn our left by outflanking us. At One in the Morning of the 29th Lord W., having received information that the Enemy were actually quitting their ground, ordered the whole British Army to march towards Coimbra. We halted one League from that place, entirely ignorant as to the route the Enemy had taken.

On the 30th we proceeded through Coimbra, and halted about half a league from it on the high Road leading to Lisbon. We ascertained this Day that the French were directing their course towards Coimbra with the utmost speed, and that their Advance Guard was only two Leagues from us. To facilitate their movements they abandoned all their wounded who were not Frenchmen, leaving them to be massacred by the Portugueze Peasantry. About seven hundred of these wretches were collected by our Rear Guard. A large part of our Army commenced its march this Day towards Lisbon, and it became pretty generally known that no further opposition would be made to the progress of the Enemy, till we should reach our lines in the Neighbourhood of the Capital.

Octr. 9th. I resume my Journal of our proceedings.—On the 1st instant at Day Break our Cavalry and those of the Enemy were drawn up in a plain opposite each other about half a league on the other side of Coimbra. No general action ensued. The skirmishing however was very sharp, and several were killed and wounded on both Sides. At length our Cavalry retired through the Town, which was almost immediately occupied by the Enemy. At Noon we received a sudden Order to march two Leagues on the high road leading to Lisbon. The Enemy evinced every disposition to press our rear, and we expected to be engaged in the course of the Afternoon. To describe the confusion of this Day is utterly impossible. The Road was so thronged with Fugitives, that it was with the utmost difficulty we reached our destination before sunset. On passing through Condixe, a considerable Town, I observed Lord W. at a window evidently affected at the Scenes of distress which were passing. It had never been apprehended that the Enemy would advance so rapidly, and therefore a great proportion of the Inhabitants had not left their Houses. In one mixed scene of confusion and misery were seen the old, the lame, and the blind, all hastening away as fast as their infirmities would allow, and all alike insensible to the blessings of French Protection which so immediately they might have enjoyed. We passed the night in an Olive Grove near the Road Side, and could distinctly hear throughout the whole of it the noise occasioned by the Fugitives. A number of Stores and a large quantity of Ammunition was destroyed at Condixe from the impossibility of removing them.

On the 2d we commenced our march before Day Break, and halted half a League on this side of Pombal amongst some Fir Trees. This day's march was most fatiguing, the distance twenty-five Miles, and the Heat more oppressive than I ever recollect to have experienced. The Fugitives on the Road were in immense numbers, but from the great width of it they were enabled to get along without incommoding the Troops. Lord W. had his Head Quarters this Evening at Leyria.

On the 3d we pursued our march five leagues further, and passing through Leyria halted among some Trees a mile and a half from that City. Here we halted on the 4th. This once populous Town was now become a Desert, not an Inhabitant remaining in it.—This day Lord W. expressed his thanks to the Troops in General Orders for their conduct at Busacos, and took that opportunity of informing them that, tho' circumstances had compelled him to abandon the Position the Enemy had in vain endeavoured to force, he yet confidently hoped to frustrate all their intentions and finally to emancipate this country from the Shackles the French were preparing to impose upon it. This Order was both politic and necessary; for, from the precipitate manner with which we had abandoned so large a track of Country, melancholy forebodings had possessed the minds of a large portion of the Army.

On the 5th we marched three Leagues, and halted near Cavalhos. Our rear Guard had this Day a very sharp skirmish with the Enemy, in which we took several Officers and sixty Men. I had a conversation with them subsequently, in which they stated their force to be less than sixty thousand Men. They expressed their astonishment at the Gallantry of the Portugueze displayed in the Action of the 27th ulto., and their wonder was not less excited at their appearance and discipline as they passed them on the Road.—They were perfectly aware of our retiring to a strong position, but remarked, whatever might be the strength of it, Massena had no alternative but must of necessity attack us. They allowed the possibility of his failure, and accompanied it with a shrue more significant than could have been expressed in any language. They admitted that since entering Portugal they had scarcely seen an Inhabitant, which was of course productive of much distress to their Army. It is said that Massena wrote to Lord W. remonstrating on the Order he had given to the People to quit their homes on the approach of the Enemy; to which his Lordship merely replied that " He regretted extremely his Excellency suffered any personal inconvenience from it."

Nothing particular occurred on the 6th. We halted near Rio Mayor, at which place Lord W. had his Head Quarters. The Enemy continued to advance, occupying the Ground as fast as we quitted it.

On the 7th we marched to Abrigada, three Leagues, and distant from Lisbon nine. On our march we fell in with a party of the Duke of Brunswick Oels Corps whose appearance excited general astonishment. Anything so fierce I never before saw; their Dress is Black, and in their Caps they wear a Death's Head.

Yesterday I consider as the most uncomfortable Day of my Life without any exception. We commenced our March at Day break having to go to Sobral, a distance of three Leagues. It blew and rained with the most dreadful violence, and in a very short time rendered the Roads nearly impassable. Unfortunately we had a Brigade of Portugueze in our Front, who, unused to march in such fearful weather, could with difficulty be persuaded to face "the pitiless pelting of the Storm." Such was our delay in consequence, that at the end of thirteen hours we found ourselves still a League from our destination. Most fortunately an order arrived for us to take up our abode for the Night in Villages near us, where by means of large Fires we succeeded in making ourselves tolerably comfortable.

This morning (9th) is showery. It is now ten o'clock, but we have as yet no orders to continue our March.

11th. In the Afternoon of the 9th we received orders to move to Villages about a Mile nearer our Position. In the course of the same Evening an express arrived, that the 14th Dragoons had been compelled to quit Abrigada about two Leagues from us by a very superior force of the Enemy. In consequence we were directed to march the next Morning (10th) to a village called Filiteira, which we reached about Noon. If possible the Day was more violent than the 8th.

Fortunately we had no Portugueze in our front, which rendered our march comparatively very short. We passed through Sobral, a Town of considerable size, in which was quartered the first Division under Lieut. Genl. Sir B. Spencer. We still remain at Filiteira, and probably shall till the French oblige us to retire to our Position, which I conceive is very near. We are scarcely two miles from Sobral. The first Division has been under Arms there the whole of the Morning, the enemy having compelled our Dragoons & Light Troops to retire there. It is impossible from the severity of the weather that they can commence Operations on any large scale at present, as the Roads are so much cut up by the Rains, that they will be unable to bring up their heavy Artillery.—This place is distant from Lisbon six leagues.

14th. On the evening of the 11th it was intended that General Spencer's Division should attack the enemy who had possession of Sobral, and our Division was in consequence ordered out on the Road leading to that place to support them in case of necessity. The night was dreadful. After remaining upwards of an hour we were directed to return to our Cantonments, the French having retired from Sobral.

The morning of the 12th proved equally violent with the preceding Night. The Commissary attached to our Division, a Young Man of most amiable manners, and a most valuable Character in his situation, was unfortunately drowned in attempting to cross a narrow Bridge. His Horse slipped and fell into the River, and he was immediately carried down by the violence of the Torrent, and seen no more. No trace could ever be discovered of his Body. Nothing material occurred this Day. There was a good deal of skirmishing in the vicinity of Sobral ; but the badness of the weather prevented any action of importance. We remained in our Cantonments in Filiteira.

Yesterday Morning broke upon us in "Thunder and Clouds & Storms :" notwithstanding we were ordered to remain under Arms. Fortunately about eight, when we received our Orders to march, the weather had cleared considerably. We ascended some Hills behind the Village we had occupied, where we remained till the Afternoon, when we were again put under Cover, it appearing evident that we should not be called upon, at least as yesterday.—The skirmishing between the Picquets was considerable, and the first fortieth Blood was drawn in the afternoon, one man on picquet being severely wounded. The 11th Portugueze Regiment, one of two attached to this Division, had an opportunity of distinguishing themselves. They had never been before engaged, and their Conduct was most heroic. They were charged by a body of French Troops which they not only gallantly resisted, but charged their Enemy in return & killed a great many of them. Col. Harvey, who commanded them and who has the merit of bringing them to their present state of discipline, was severely wounded. The privation of his services is considered a great publick loss

This day all remains quiet. The enemy show themselves in force on the opposite Hills, but do not manifest any disposition to advance. The weather is at present fine, but does not appear entirely settled. Should it continue favourable, they must of necessity commence their operations, as the exhausted state of the Country they have passed through will not admit of delay.

15th. Yesterday at noon a very smart skirmish took place in which the 71st was principally engaged. They maintained the high Character which has so long distinguished them. It was an experiment on the part of the Enemy which entirely failed. They lost several Officers and two Hundred Men. Our loss was about fifty. In the Evening an Aide du Camp of Genl. Miller, who has a command in the Portugueze service, passed through here on his way to Head Quarters from Coimbra. He represents that place in possession of the Portugueze, Genl. M. being there with five thousand Men. They found there four thousand sick and wounded French, who were sent down to Oporto.

The whole of this Day has been perfectly quiet, but doubtless the Enemy has been preparing for the Attack which from their desperate situation cannot be long delayed. The weather continues unfavourable.

18th. Since the last Date nothing material has occurred; indeed scarcely a shot has been fired. The Weather has become much finer, and the Enemy as well as ourselves have been busy in throwing up Works. Our Advance Posts are very near each other. We observe their Generals constantly reconnoitring. One of them a few days since, advanced too near and was fired at from one of the Batteries. He was killed by the first Shot. His name is said to be La Croix or St. Croix, an Officer of considerable eminence.

Many opinions are formed as to the cause of the delay of the Enemy in attacking us. The most probable one is that they are waiting for reinforcements. Deserters say that the Ninth Corps is expected in a few days, and that operations will not commence till their arrival.

21st. Scarcely a single shot has been fired since the last date. Our advanced Posts and those of the enemy are within three hundred yards of each other. It was for several days the practice of the men of both Armies to meet in the same Vineyards in the Valleys, and even to talk and shake hands with each other. This has however very properly been put a stop to, it being very justly considered that the Simplicity of our Fellows was no match for the Cunning of a Frenchman. Desertions from the enemy are frequent—on an average not less than fifty a Day. They all concur in stating their extreme want of Provisions; and indeed the voracity with which they devour anything given them is ample Confirmation of the truth of their Statement.

I this day visited an immense Fort which is situated about Midway between the sea and the Tagus. It is a most stupendous Work, and commands the admiration of all Military Men. The View from it is very extensive; the sea and the

Tagus can be distinctly seen. From its great height, it has the advantage of exposing all the movements of the Enemy.

The Marquis Romana with ten thousand Men arrived in the Neighbourhood Yesterday. From the emulation existing between the Spaniards and the Portugueze much is expected from these Troops.

25th. We remain as quiet as if we had not an Enemy within an hundred miles of us. Marshal Ney's Corps is said to be gone to the Rear to open a communication with Almeida, and the Enemy are busily employed in throwing a Bridge across the Tagus near Santarem for the purpose of procuring Provisions from the Alentejo side. Unfortunately their having possession of Villa Franca prevents our Gun Boats from getting up and impeding them. It is thought however, that some Dash will yet be done by the Navy to prevent their accomplishing their object.

The whole of the Enemy's Picquets are now French, and they keep so vigilant a look out, that the Germans and other Foreign Troops find it almost impossible to desert; consequently but few come in.

29th. Still no movement on either Side. Our men are constantly employed in throwing up works, making entrenchments,&c.,thus strengthening what was before considered almost impregnable. The weather has today a very threatening appearance. Should the Rain set, in the Enemy will suffer infinitely more than ourselves from it. A few Mornings since we were very much astonished here at the excessively loud roaring of the Sea, and it appears that at the same time the People at Lisbon were very much alarmed by the shock of an Earthquake, which does not appear however to have done any particular injury.

Novr. 3d. The Enemy manifest no intention of either advancing or retiring. We know not by what means they have been able to subsist themselves so long, but we trust they will ere long be compelled to attack us or retreat. There is scarcely a possibility of their succeeding in the former ; and if they attempt the latter they will doubtless suffer considerably. Massena has failed in redeeming the pledge he made to his Troops to be in Lisbon by the 1st of this Month, and it is probable he has postponed his intention sine die. The weather is very unpleasant, being extremely cold, attended frequently with rain. The place we are in is most wretched, and furnishes no one species of comfort. Scarcely a house in the whole Village is weatherproof.

6th. This Morning we distinctly saw a number of General & other Officers busily employed in reconnoitring our Position. They came very near, but were not fired at. From the richness of Uniform, the number of Officers attending and the strength of the Escort, there is no doubt that it was Massena himself. No idea however is entertained that they will venture to attack us.

9th. The Day before yesterday Marshal Beresford was installed a Knight of the Bath at the Palace at Mafra. This circumstance may be considered as an Era in Military History. Lord Wellington having availed himself of the opportunity to give a splendid Dinner to two hundred People, in the Evening there was a Ball and Supper to which a proportion of the Officers of the Army were invited. Besides Lord Wellington & General Beresford, most of the General Officers were present. Several of the Regency and Ministers of State, with Adml. Berkely and Family, and several Families of the first distinction from Lisbon attended ; also the Marquis Romana with other Spanish General Officers, and at least four or five hundred Officers of inferior Rank of the Spanish, Portugueze and British Armies. Lord W. was in the highest Spirits. He withdrew privately about Midnight, and the whole had retired soon after two o'Clock in the Morning. It was difficult to conceive at the Moment that we were before an Enemy, everything being conducted in the same manner as if it were in a Country in a state of profound Peace.

The Palace at Mafra is a most magnificent pile of building, and in every respect worthy of being a Royal Residence. It was dark when we arrived there, which prevented our seeing more of it than the Rooms that were thrown open ; and its distance from this part of the Position, renders it difficult to go there by Day for the purpose of viewing it with that attention it is undoubtedly deserving of.

The weather is bad, and appears to be breaking. All ideas of taking the Field seem to be abandoned, as the Tents which were served out are ordered again to be returned into Store. The Enemy remain in the same Positions they have for some time occupied.

21st. On the Evening of the 14th we observed that the Enemy made much larger Fires than usual, which gave reason to believe they were about retreating. Our ideas were well founded, as on the Morning of the 15th when Day broke not one of them was to be seen. Lord W. in consequence ordered forward immediately the Dragoons and Light Division, supported by the First and Second Divisions. On the 17th, it being considered probable that our Division would not march for some Days, I took the advantage of our proximity to Lisbon, being only six Leagues, to go there, from whence I returned this Day. I found the people there, so far as I could observe, generally dissatisfied that the French had got away. They appeared to think that we should have attacked them, and in their opinion the Portugueze Troops alone were amply sufficient to have annihilated them. The Enemy on their retreat took the direction of Santarem, where they still remain, but whether from choice or necessity is uncertain. It is supposed that they are detained there in consequence of some Bridges being carried away by the late very heavy Rains having swelled the Rivers. A variety of Prisoners have already fallen into our Hands. The 40th Regiment left Palmira on Sunday Morning the 19th, and marched to Alenquer, a Town of considerable size, and where it seems for some time Massena had his Head Quarters.   Yesterday they came to another large Town called Azemboja where they still remain, and in which place I found them this Morning on joining.   I came here by way of Villa Franca, which formed the advance of the French Army.   From that town to this, a distance of three Leagues, is exhibited one melancholy scene of desolation.   The Skeletons of the Houses only remain, and the Roads are strewn with the Carcases of dead Animals.

26th.   We still remain at Azemboja, and the enemy continue at Santarem.   Lord W.'s Head Quarters are at Cartajo, about two leagues on this side of Santarem and the same distance from this place.   Of the minor movements of the Enemy we know nothing.   Their communication with the Alemtejo is prevented by Genl. Hill, who crossed the River some days since with the whole of his Division.   This Town is nearly two Miles from the Tagus, and separated from it by a flat Marsh which in the months of August, September, and October, must render it in my opinion little less unwholesome than the Island of Walcheren.

This is generally and justly considered one of the most sickening Campaigns in Military History ; notwithstanding the advanced Season of the Year, there being no probability of an early conclusion to it.   A great portion of the Officers of the British Army are disgusted with it, as the Gazette some few Months hence will, I conceive, abundantly evince.

The French Prisoners brought in unanimously concur in stating that the Enemy have received large reinforcements, and with all the insolence of the French Character they tell us a very short time will elapse before we are driven into the Sea.   It may here be worthy of remark, that in passing through Alenquer (a Town of considerable size, which for some time was Massena's Head Quarters) the British Officer observed on the house he occupied written in large Letters—Le logement du Prince d'Esling ; he immediately inscribed under it—

" Qui a fait plus de bruit au battant la caisse qu'en betrant les Anglais." It is said that Massena commenced his military career as a Drummer.

December 5th. The respective Armies remain in the same positions as on the last Date. The situation is so far advantageous for ourselves, as the troops are more cheaply and expeditiously supplied by means of Boats, the greater part of our army being in the vicinity of the Tagus.

I yesterday rode to the advance, a distance of about twelve or fifteen miles from hence. I remained an hour within Pistol Shot of their Centinels, but no Shots are now ever exchanged. The Enemy are intrenching themselves as strongly as possible at Santarem, from which it would appear they have no intention of abandoning the Position they at present hold.

English papers received yesterday to the 7th ulto. confirm the unpleasant intelligence of the King's Malady. On the supposition that it may continue, many Speculations are afloat. It is conjectured by several, that in the event of a Regency there will be an entire change in the policy hitherto observed towards the Peninsula. Most people however seem to think, that, should a British Force continue here, no set of Ministers would dare to displace Lord Wellington, as from his deserved popularity and local knowledge such a change would not fail to excite the utmost discontent among the British and despondency among the Portugueze Troops. As the Wind has now been fair several Days, we may very soon expect intelligence of a much later date.

14th. Our news from England does not come later than the 27th Ulto., at which time nothing had been done with respect to a Regency. Whoever may be Ministers, I have not a doubt that the same policy will be pursued towards this Country. In the meantime the Enemy continue to maintain themselves at Santarem, and from thence to Thomar and Leyria. Lord Wellington amuses himself with hunting and shooting, and it is said that a few days since in the ardour of the chace he and Massena were very near coming upon each other. The rides in this neighbourhood are excellent. There are several beautiful Quintas within a short distance, but it is melancholy to observe the devastation committed on them by the Enemy, every House exhibiting proof of the most wanton and unprofitable barbarity. The Murders they have perpetrated on the unfortunate Peasantry, instigated it is supposed by disappointed Avarice, are horrible & scarcely to be credited.

26th. A second journey to Lisbon, where I remained three or four Days, afforded me an opportunity of observing a great change in the Sentiments of the People. They now appear to think that Lord W. was right in not risking an attack on the Enemy. The utmost tranquillity prevails there, and business and amusement are carried on and pursued with as much avidity as if the Country were in a state of profound peace. Nothing new on the part of the Enemy. It is rumoured Lord W. means to move the Army somewhat nearer Lisbon for the purpose of facilitating the supplies.

31st. An Aide du Camp of Massena's has been taken with despatches on his way to Almeida. As he was disguised when taken, he was liable according to the Laws of war to be shot as a spy. His Life was offered him on condition of making a full disclosure of everything he knew. The information gained from him of course has not transpired; but it is supposed to be important, as Genl. Hill made a sudden movement with his Division towards Abrantes, and Sir Stapleton Cotton who was at Lisbon on the point of embarking for England has joined the Army to assume again the Command of the Cavalry.

[1811]
[JAN.] January 13th. Another Fortnight has elapsed without anything particular having occurred. It is confidently stated that Reinforcements to an immense amount are on their way to join Massena, but it would seem as if Lord W. did not

expect operations would speedily commence, as Sir S. Cotton and other General Officers are proceeding to England.

20th. We were last night awoke at midnight with an Order to pack the baggage, and be in readiness to march at a Moment's Notice. At nine o'Clock this morning, however, intelligence arrived from Head Quarters that this precaution was no longer necessary. It seems the Enemy entered Rio Mayor yesterday evening in force, & it was deemed likely that they were about to advance to their old ground. They moved back again however towards Leyria in the course of the Night, and in consequence the bustle amongst us subsided.

25th. The utmost tranquillity again prevails ; the 9th Corps has joined Massena, but it is probable that his whole force is not at present more than it was when he first entered Portugal.

The Marquis Romana died the day before yesterday at Head Quarters ; his death adds another to the many instances of the awful uncertainty of Human Life. On the 23rd Inst. his Baggage passed thro' this place, and he was to have followed it as yesterday ; it being his intention to have proceeded to the Alemtejo with his Army to increase the Allied force in that Quarter, under the apprehension that Mortier with the 5th Corps was about to invade that Province. A few hours after his Baggage had set out he was seized with spasms in his stomach & almost immediately expired. His zeal in the cause was unquestionable, but his Talents were considered below par.

February 1. This Morning one of the Brunswick Corps was shot here for attempting to desert to the Enemy. So many of these men have lately been guilty of the same Crime, that Lord W. found it necessary to remove them from the position they occupied in front. They are now quartered in this place. Their defection will furnish matter of great triumph to the malicious Soul of Cobbett,

In the late reconnoissance at Rio Mayor a French, General Officer was certainly wounded in the Head. The Deserters say that it was Junot, and that he has since been buried at Thomar, the wound having proved mortal.

4th. Last Night about twelve o'Clock we felt distinctly the Shock of an Earthquake, and Daylight this Morning presented us the novel appearance of the immense flat between this place & the Tagus in a complete state of inundation. The General Officer wounded at Rio Mayor was Junot. A letter from his lady written from Ciudad Rodrigo announcing her happy accouchement was intercepted & brought to Lord W. There being nothing of a political nature in it, the latter transmitted it to its destination. This piece of politeness was acknowledged by Junot in a letter to Lord W. in which he states that in the skirmish at Rio Mayor he was " Grievement blessè."

Preparations are making at Lisbon for the reception of a great many Regiments from England & Sicily, and it is confidently said that Lord W. will on their arrival, or as soon after as the weather will permit, act on the offensive. This appears to be the general wish ; the whole Army is tired of the late inactivity. If something is not done soon, it is probable the New Ministers will put a stop to all ulterior intentions by withdrawing the Army from the Peninsula. Their Organ, the *Morning Chronicle*, appears to be feeling the public Pulse on the subject. Such a proceeding would blot the Page of History, and should only be recorded as a memento of the infamy of those who could recommend and adopt such a measure.

18. A continuance of Southerly Winds has prevented our receiving any intelligence from England for a considerable time. The same cause probably has operated against the arrival of the expected reinforcements. In the mean time all remains quiet on this side the Tagus. The 5th Corps of

[1811]
[FEBR.] the French Army under Mortier on the other side has taken Olivenza, & besieged or rather invested Badajos. The Garrison made a Sortie a few days since, destroyed the Enemy's works, & killed twelve hundred ; their own loss was severe. General Foix, returning from Paris to the Head Quarters of Massena a short time since, with an Escort of two thousand Infantry and a thousand Cavalry, had his Rear Guard attacked by a Colonel Miller with only Eighty of the Ordinanza with him. It is worthy of record, that with this small force he captured a great part of the Baggage and killed two hundred & seven Men, among whom was the Colonel of the 70th Regiment. Castanos is appointed to succeed the Marquis Romana. This appointment has given great satisfaction.

[MARCH] March 1. Since my last date we have papers to the 2nd Ulto., at which time the Regency Bill had not passed both Houses. Reinforcements to a large amount are coming out, which will, it is generally supposed, render Lord W. sufficiently strong to enable him to commence offensive Operations with advantage. At all events it appears impossible that the Enemy can remain long in their present Position : there are the most unquestionable proofs of them at present undergoing the severest privations, and two French Officers who passed through this place Prisoners a few days since unequivocally stated that the French Army was too weak to hazard the attempt of forcing the Lines. Indeed they avowed their opinion that Portugal would not be conquered now or at any other time ; and this idea they principally founded on the extraordinary devotion of the lower Orders to their Country, & consequent detestation of their Invaders. And indeed it is impossible not to admire this people. On the approach of the enemy they instantly pack up their little all, and abandon their Homes with a cheerfulness almost inconceivable.—In the different Towns and Villages where there are Military, subscriptions have been received by which means several thousand of them are daily provided with an excellent Dinner,

In the meantime the Spanish Troops which marched from this Neighbourhood a few weeks since have been surprised by the Enemy near Badajos, who killed about two thousand of them ; the rest dispersed in all directions, leaving behind them the whole of their Baggage, and every piece of their Artillery. They have now, I believe, no regular Army, but they can do an infinite deal more mischief to the Enemy by confining themselves to a desultory mode of warfare, such as the intercepting of small Parties, Convoys, etc. Badajos has not yet fallen, but it is not now expected to hold out long.

7th. On the evening of the 4th Orders were received for the 4th Division to march the following Morning & occupy Cantonments in the neighbourhood of Cartaxo ; the 3d Divn. was directed to remove from Alemquer & take up our Quarters at Azemboja ; these movements were in consequence of Lord W. receiving information that a variety of circumstances indicated an early movement on the part of the Enemy. His conjectures were not ill-founded, as favoured by the obscurity of Night, they abandoned their position about eight o'clock on the evening of the 5th. The next Morning all the British Army was in Motion ; the Dragoons & Light Division went in pursuit of the Enemy ; the 1st, 3d, & 4th Divisions marched to Santarem, where we remained last night. It is a town of very considerable size, but exhibits a melancholy instance of French Barbarism ; the Churches in particular have suffered the most unheard of devastation ; one only was spared, and that had been converted into a regular Theatre, where, so late as Sunday evening last, the triumphal entry of the French Army into Lisbon was represented. The Position they occupied here is certainly one of the finest in Portugal.—It appearing that they had commenced their retreat in two columns, the one by Torres Novas & the other by Golgão, Lord W. likewise has divided his force in pursuit of them. We arrived at the latter place this day, but I have not yet been able to ascertain whether the Enemy (who quitted this Village this morning at eight o'clock) are retreating in the direction of Thomar, or have crossed the Zezere and propose going by Castel Branco. Hitherto we have made but few Prisoners. Lord W. is with that part of the Army following them by the way of Torres Novas.

12th. On the 8th we marched to Thomar, which place the Enemy had quitted the same Morning. We found that their whole force was retreating in the direction of Coimbra. We halted on the 9th, on which Day it was generally understood, & indeed certainly intended, that our Division, with the Second, & a Brigade of Cavalry, should proceed into the Alemtejo, and attack Mortier at present investing Badajos. This arrangement was however altered, an Order arriving in the Night for our marching the next Morning in the direction of Pombal, the Enemy having shewn themselves there in great force, & with an apparent intention of making a resolute defence there, it being a considerable Depot for their stores. We halted for the Night on the side of a Hill about three Leagues from Thomar. On the following morning (the 11th) we proceeded on our way to Pombal, distant upwards of five Leagues. On our route we heard the Enemy were in a strong Position with every apparent intention of defending it. The different Divisions were directed to march as quick as possible, as Lord W. was most anxious to attack them before Sunset. The length of the March & the badness of the Roads rendered this impracticable ; the attack was therefore deferred till this Morning, and the necessary orders given for carrying it into execution at Day Break. The Town of Pombal was carried very gallantly yesterday by the Dragoons & Light Brigade ; it being however under the Fire of the Enemy's Artillery, they were compelled to evacuate it. In the Evening the Enemy took up a Position on some heights on the right Hand of the great Road leading to Coimbra. Lord W. took up his position immediately opposite to them. Between the two Armies was a flat about half a mile in breadth and a

River waist high running in the centre of it. The crossing of this, it was generally conceived, would occasion much loss in our Army, it being so completely commanded by the enemy's Artillery. This loss however we had not to sustain, as at Daybreak we found the Foe had disappeared. We consequently lost no time in pursuing them. We came up with them about a league & a half from Pombal, when the Army was formed for a regular attack, which they again evaded by a precipitate flight. There was however a most beautiful affair of Posts, in which the Enemy lost several hundred in killed, wounded & Prisoners; our loss was about a hundred. Lord W's dispositions for the attack to-day excited the greatest admiration throughout the Army, & prove him to be a consummate General. We have no means of ascertaining the force of the enemy, but it is supposed it is only a Rear Guard consisting of about fifteen thousand men, and, as we hear, all French.—They regularly burn to the Ground every place they pass through. In following them we find each Town & Village a heap of smoking ruins. Our halt this night is near Redinha above three Leagues from Condexa, but I do not at present know how far the enemy are in advance of us.

14th. The Enemy were so strongly entrenched in Condexa yesterday that it was not deemed prudent to attack them. We halted above a League from that place & could distinctly see the Town burning the whole day. In the afternoon they retired, taking the direction of the Ponte de Murcella. The Light Division took up a Position on the Enemy's side of the Town; it was feared the French would make a forced march in the night and pass the Ponte de Murcella without further opposition. At Daylight this Morning we commenced our March & passed through Condexa; not a solitary House remained that was not burnt to the Ground. It was a beautiful Town when we were last here. We had not got a mile from Condexa when a sharp firing commenced in our front An Order was received for our Division to march to Espinhal, where we arrived this evening; it is possible there may be a double Meaning in this Movement. It is pretty certain that we are destined for the Alemtejo, this place being in the high Road from the Ponte de Murcella to Thomar & distant from the latter place eight leagues ; there is little doubt but we shall commence our march for Thomar to-morrow Morning. At the same time by this movement we threaten the Enemy's left Flank. Tho' distant from the Scene of Action we heard the firing distinctly the whole Day ; the carnage must have been dreadful ; we have not the possibility of knowing the extent of our loss , but I think it may be fairly estimated at a thousand men. We had the satisfaction of knowing however that our brave fellows were compelling their Enemy to retire.

16th. Yesterday Afternoon we received an Order to march in the direction of Thomar, which place we were to have reached this Evening, but the distance (eight Leagues) prevented us; we have halted for the night at or rather in the vicinity of a small Village called Venda Nova, and to-morrow we pursue our march to Tancos, where it is intended we shall cross the Tagus. It will be a week before we reach the Enemy, and ere that period it is to be feared Badajos may have fallen. Lord W., after pursuing his Foe to a certain point, proposes assuming the command of the British force in the Alemtejo.

The wretched Inhabitants are returning to their destroyed dwellings. They could by no means understand our retrograde movement of this Day, and it was with difficulty we could persuade them that the French were not at our heels. The enormities committed on the property and Persons of these poor People by the Enemy can scarcely be recited with the expectation of gaining belief. The entire destruction of the different Towns and Villages they have lately passed through renders it probable that they have no intention of ever again invading the Country, but the Ruin and Devastation they have occasioned cannot be entirely effaced in a less period than half a Century.

18th. Early yesterday morning we reached Thomar where we halted for the Day; on our arrival there we had the mortification to learn that Badajos surrendered on the 10th. Whatever were the intentions of Lord W., they are I suppose suspended for the present; in the meantime Marshal Beresford who commands on this side of the water has directed the troops to march in the direction of Portalegre, doubtless with a view to covering the Alemtejo, which may be said in some degree to be threatened by Mortier. Our march to-day was only three leagues We halted for the Night in the vicinity of a small Village immediately on the Banks of the Tagus called Arripiada; the Enemy have never had footing in it, but it is not sufficiently capacious to accommodate the Troops.

We are without news from the Army, but we have learned that notwithstanding the very heavy firing on the 13th our loss did not exceed one hundred and fifty men.

20th. Yesterday Morning we commenced our march at Daylight; our Route lay through a difficult but most picturesque Country along the Banks of the Tagus. We halted for the Night in the Neighbourhood of a village immediately opposite Abrantes; this Day we have marched four Leagues, and to our great surprise are in houses in a miserable village called Gavão; we are still Eight Leagues from Portalegre. On our arrival there it is probable we shall know something respecting our final destination. It is most desirable that the troops should have a few Days' rest before they again encounter their Enemy. A March of between two and three hundred miles necessarily occasions a great wear and tear in the Appointments of Soldiers.

24th. On the 21st we marched five Leagues and halted at a place called Alpaltrão, sufficiently large to accommodate the Division; the following day we reached Portalegre, a Town of considerable size. Here we had the mortification to learn that the enemy had taken Campo Mayor. Papers from England to the 6th Inst. announced to us the Regent's intention of pursuing the War in the Peninsular with Vigour. The exhausted state of the Troops and the want of Shoes rendered it necessary for the Division to halt the 23d. Portalegre has a beautiful Cathedral, and the principal Cloth Manufactory of the Kingdom is likewise there.

This day we marched Four leagues to Arronches; Marshal Beresford with the 2d Division had quitted it before our arrival. Campo Mayor is distant from hence only four Leagues ; the Enemy have four thousand Troops there, and hopes are entertained that a part of our force may get between them and Badajos & cut them off.—We have no Accts. from Lord Wellington.

26th. We left Arronches at daybreak yesterday Morning and arrived before Campo Mayor by a circuitous route about two in the Afternoon. We found the enemy had quitted it at Noon, and that they were closely pursued by our Dragoons. It is impossible to describe the Joy of the Inhabitants as we passed the Town ; they hailed us with the loudest acclamations. We had not proceeded two miles further before a very different Scene presented itself ; the road was strewn with the dead and dying. At the end of a long League from the Town we received Orders to return to Campo Mayor. The Enemy were pursued by a part of the 13th Dragoons to the very Walls of Badajos. In their Confusion they abandoned everything, but unfortunately, the 13th not being supported by Infantry, they were enabled to remove their Artillery &c., &c., afterwards. One Howitzer & many Prisoners remained in our possession & the Enemy's loss in killed was very great ; on our side we lost three Officers & about fifty Men.—There is nothing indicating a probability of our quitting this place ; it is supposed that Marshal Beresford waits for instructions from Lord Wellington. In the mean time he has taken up his Quarters at Elvas.

29th. We are anxiously waiting for news from the Army under Lord Wellington ; it is near a Fortnight since we have had any Acct. of it ; in the mean time we remain here in a state of profound inactivity ; it appears that the 13th Dragoons in pursuing the Enemy the other Evening took sixteen pieces of Cannon, all their Baggage and upwards of a thousand Prisoners, but from some strange infatuation the heavy Dragoons & Infantry not being allowed to follow them they were enabled again to take possession of all they had lost and bear it in safety to Badajos. Complaints are deep and general on the occasion against the Marshal, and it is very probable the Affair will yet cause much stir.

[APRIL] Apr. 2d. Yesterday morning we marched from Campo Mayor to Elvas, where we occupy the Quarters vacated by the 2d Division who are gone to Villa Vicosa. The utmost secrecy as to our future Operations is observed ; preparations however on a large scale are making for a siege, which it is supposed can only be for the purposes of attacking Badajos.

The number of Military here is about fifteen thousand. These with the inhabitants and a crowd of fugitives have filled the Town to excess. Every Article is in consequence enormously high.

The last accts. from Lord W. are of the 25th Ulto., at which time his advanced Guard was at Celerico ; he had made many Prisoners.

6th. We quitted Elvas on the morning of the 4th Inst., and encamped the same day in the neighbourhood of Jerumenha. We wait here till the 2d Division shall have passed the Guadiana ; the River is not at present fordable, & the floating Bridge is very incomplete ; in all probability we shall not get across before to-morrow Morning. In the meantime we are in the most perfect ignorance of the movements of the Enemy ; we do not even know whether or not they are in possession of Olivenza, tho' it is only two Leagues from us. We are in hopes that Lord W. will almost immediately be with us, accts. from Head Quarters stating that the Enemy have been dispossessed of Guarda, and that they have been compelled to retire to the other side of the Coa, so that the campaign in the North of Portugal may be considered as terminated. The whole Army here long for the presence of the Comr. of the Forces, so unbounded is their confidence in him; and indeed he does appear to leave far behind him all his Competitors for Military Fame.

10th. At one in the morning of the 7th we crossed the Guadiana, and proceeded about half a League on the Road leading to Olivenza. Our entrance into Spain was marked by an event sufficiently calamitous, when it is considered it might have been avoided by Common Prudence. We had just laid down after reaching our halting ground on the Morning of the 7th when we were alarmed by a sharp firing in the midst of the Camp; the confusion was general, most of the men being in a sound sleep. The cause of the Alarm was a Party of French Dragoons who had forced our Picquets, and had the audacity to come to the very confines of our Camp; fortunately they were not aware of our confusion and they retired. We had however the mortification to learn very soon that they surprised two Squadrons of the 13th Dragoons, & that they had taken them off in triumph to Olivenza. This unfortunate business is said to be wholly attributable to the Officer commanding that portion of the Cavalry who tho' in the most advanced post of the Army had suffered his men to unbridle, and they were thus rendered incapable of resistance.—We remained on the same ground the whole of that Day and the 8th, during which time the other part of the Army, Artillery, Stores, Baggage, etc., etc., were crossing the river. Yesterday morning we proceeded on the Road towards Olivenza, and halted about a Mile from the Town. Marshal Beresford sent in a Flag of Truce offering Terms, which were rejected by the Garrison, tho' they do not amount to four hundred men. Some very extraordinary reason must be the cause of the enemy leaving so inefficient a force. The Marshal has sent to Elvas for heavy Artillery for the purpose of making a breaching Battery, & taking it by Storm, should they be so imprudent as to push things to that extremity. It appears extremely odd that the possibility not to say probability, of their refusing to deliver up the Garrison should not have been earlier taken into Acct., and the Battering Train on the spot; there does appear however that there is a fatality attending the Operations of this Army which forms a striking Contrast with the energy and foresight displayed in every movement by the troops under Lord W. Fortunately the weather since last night has assumed an appearance which promises to continue fine; it has been for several days dreadful, & the sufferings & hardships of the Troops have in consequence been extreme.—Accts. have reached us from Lord Wellington to the 3d on which Day he crossed the Coa, and attacked the enemy, compelling them to retreat with the loss of upwards of a thousand Men.

12th. Yesterday passed without any particular occurrence. The siege is left to our Division (the 4th), the 2d & a Division of Portugueze having marched to Valverde, a short distance from hence, to act as a Corps of observation. Last Night the Trenches were opened; the Enemy kept up a smart Fire during the Night; the only casualty however was the loss of one of the Brunswick Corps, whose Head was carried clean off by a Cannon Shot. It is hoped that in the course of this Night the breaching Battery will be completed & the Guns mounted by Daylight ready to open; its contiguity to the Town will make the breach to be effected in a very short time tho' it is probable they will capitulate before even that shall be effected.

13th. The breaching Battery is made in an old Redoubt about two hundred and sixty yards from the Town; it will be completed this Night, but could not be finished sooner from the great difficulty found in removing the Angle, where it will be necessary for the guns to enter, the Gate leading into it being exposed to the Enemy's Fire. The twenty-four

Pounders are to open in the Morning ; it is intended to use
every caution not to injure the Town. As soon as Olivenza
falls, it is understood we shall commence the siege of Badajos,
which is said to contain a Garrison of only Seven hundred
men ; we shall however find more annoyance there, as it is
much better supplied with Artillery.

17. The Battery was completed on the night of the 13th,
but on bringing up the Guns the entrance was found to be too
narrow : we had therefore the mortification of being obliged to
wait another 24 hours. This was remedied the following
Night & at Daylight yesterday the Battery was ready to open.
At half past five a Flag of Truce was sent in offering them
the honours of war ; which they rejected ; the Guns immediately
opened. At noon they sent out offering to deliver up the
place, provided they were allowed to go to France as Prisoners
of War, not to serve till regularly exchanged ; they were
answered, that as they had given us the trouble of erecting
and opening our Batteries, they must now surrender at
discretion. A second message was then received from them
requesting the terms offered them in the Morning : the only
reply was a renewal of the Firing. Finding us determined
and aware that a very short time would suffice to render the
breach practicable, they surrendered at discretion, and about
two o'Clock a portion of our Troops marched in, when 21
Officers and upwards of four hundred Men were made
Prisoners. We were received by the Inhabitants with the
loudest acclamations. Notwithstanding the Enemy kept up
an incessant Fire Night and Day upon our working parties,
our Casualties were only four killed & eight wounded. The
expectation of marching immediately upon Badajos was general.
To our surprise however we yesterday received Orders to
proceed in the direction of Santa Marta which is on the high
Road to Seville, & distant from Olivenza seven Leagues.
We arrived in the neighbourhood of the former place this
Morning, when we found directions to wait here till further

Orders. Marshal Beresford is in front with the Cavalry and
2d Division, but we are entirely ignorant of his plans and
intentions. We have passed through several Spanish Towns
and Villages, and they all bear evident marks of having enjoyed
the blessings of French protection ; the Country between this
& Olivenza is for the most part entirely barren.

20th. We remained encamped near Santa Marta till this
morning, when we received Orders to retrograde in the
direction of Olivenza ; we have halted for the present at a
Town called Almandhral situated about half way between
those two places. It is conjectured we are immediately going
to invest Badajos. Lord W. reaches Elvas this Evening ;
under his auspices the Siege will doubtless be vigourously
conducted.

The 17th Dragoons had an opportunity a few days ago of
being revenged on the very troops who surprised their Squadron
near Jerumenha ; they came up with them near Zafra, and
destroyed & took prisoners nearly two hundred of them.

We have little news of the Army in the North ; it appears
our Advance have passed Ciudad Rodrigo, & that Almeida is
invested.

22d. Yesterday morning we left Alamandhral, & marched
to Valverde, which is distant from Badajos about four Leagues;
we hope to remain here till everything is ready to commence
the siege. The 16th of this Month was set apart at Lisbon
for a solemn Jubilee to celebrate the entire expulsion of the
Enemy from Portugal. It is impossible not to remark a great
Apathy amongst the Spaniards, when compared with the
extraordinary devotion to the cause of the Country pervading
the Breasts of the lower orders in Portugal.

25th. We received our Orders to quit Valverde at Noon
on the 23rd for the purpose of crossing the River at Jerumenha,
the latter place not being large enough to accommodate the
Brigade. Our Regiment remained in a small Village on this

side of the water, intending to follow the Brigade to Elvas the following day. This plan was frustrated by the Bridge being carried away, the heavy Rains we have lately had having swollen the River to an unusual height. We know not what was the intention of our going towards Elvas, & we are equally ignorant what we are now going to do. Yesterday Afternoon we were directed to march to Olivenza, and this morning we proceeded from that place to Valverde, where we remain this Night, and go on to-morrow to Talavera Real, & from thence it is supposed to Merida, where we shall again meet our Brigade ; in the mean time we are attached to the Light Brigade under Genl. Alten. The weather has been for some time & still is very unfavourable for carrying on the Siege ; it is to be hoped on the settling of the fine weather everything will be ready for conducting it vigorously.

27th. We reached Talavera yesterday Afternoon after a fatiguing March of five Leagues through a most barren Country. We have as yet no orders to proceed further. This place is called Talavera la Real to distinguish it from Talavera de la Reyna where Lord Wellington gained his celebrated Victory.—It would appear as if the principal seat of warfare will be in the North, Lord W. having left us again to join the Army there.

May 2d. On the 28th Ulto. we quitted Talavera, and proceeded to a village called Lobon, two Leagues further on the Merida road ; we halted there till yesterday morning, when we reached Merida, where we crossed the Guadiana, and to-day came to a small Town called La Puebla immediately opposite to Lobon. The two other Regiments of the Brigade are quartered in Montejo about half a Mile from hence. We expect to remain here till the commencement of the siege ; the accommodation is better than we have for a long time experienced.

Merida is a town of very great antiquity ; the scientific Antiquarian will find in it ample scope for his research ;

amongst other ancient Structures is a very fine Aqueduct built
by the Saracens, & the remains of a large Roman Amphi-
theatre, which have since been converted into a Place del
Toros or place for Bull-fighting, but is now in Ruins.

4th.   We remain in La Puebla without any intimation as
to the probability or improbability of an early removal.   We
are so comfortable here that all, Officers & Men, are anxious
to stay.   The German Brigade marched last night from
Talavera to commence the investment of Badajos.   It is
possible we are to form a Corps of observation ; at all events
we are fortunate in getting to this Side of the River, as the
principal Operations will be carried on on the other.   I call it
fortunate, because there is so much fatigue and so little glory
attending a besieging Army, that it is rarely one meets a
Military Man anxious to be engaged in such a service.

6th.   It would appear as if the Siege was on the point of
commencing ; the Town is completely invested on the South
Side of the Guadiana, and we expect to march to-morrow or
the day after at farthest to complete the investment.   In the
mean time we are entirely separated from our Division.   The
Fusiliers & Portugueze Brigade marched this Morning from
Merida in the direction of Badajos, to take a part in the
operations to be carried on on the other side.   A most obstinate
defence is expected from the Enemy ; nevertheless we hope to
be in possession of the Town by the 4th of June next.

9th.   We quitted La Puebla early on the morning of the
7th, & bivouacked that Night in a wood.   Yesterday about
ten o'clock we arrived on our ground in front of Fort
St. Christoval, a work of some strength on the North side of
the Guadiana, & from its Situation commanding the Town.
The Enemy for sometime disputed some heights near it, but
were at length compelled to retire into the Fort.   They
communicate with the town by means of the Bridge.   Last
night we broke ground for the purpose of erecting a Battery

to dislodge the Enemy from the Fort; at the same time our
Friends on the opposite Side of the water commenced their
operations. The Siege appears to be well begun. The Fire
from the Enemy's guns has been very severe; the loss of the
Brigade on this side of the River already amounts to about
eight Men killed & several Officers & fifty Men wounded.
Our situation is a most unpleasant one; the weather is
extremely hot, and we have not the smallest possible Cover;
we consequently look forward with much anxiety to the
completion of the Siege.

11th. The working Parties resumed their operations on
the night of the 9th. Its proximity to the Enemy's work is
considered as rendering it a most daring undertaking to break
ground so near them. It would appear that they dread our
getting possession of it, and yesterday morng. soon after Daylight they made a most serious effort to dislodge us from it.
They succeeded in getting possession of it for a moment, &
were proceeding to destroy the Work when they were charged
by the Picquets & compelled to retreat. Unfortunately our
Troops pursued them with their wonted ardour to the very
Walls, where they were exposed to a most destructive Fire of
Shell Shot and Musquetry; notwithstanding with a very
inferior force they completely routed their Enemy. Tho'
the affair was but of short duration, the Brigade lost four
hundred Men, of which two hundred were of the 40th; the
loss of Officers was also very great; we had eight wounded,
among whom my two Messmates, the Lieut.-Col. & Major,
were severely handled: it was one of the most painful Days of
my Life.

This Day our Battery opened, but the Enemy have been
able to bring so many Guns to bear upon it that it cannot act
with much effect, & indeed there is reason to fear they will
be enabled to dismantle it; we have not found the co-opera-
tion we expected from the Army on the other Side of the Water.

13. As was apprehended, the Guns were completely silenced before the Evening of the 11th. Little has been done since, and we are all in a complete state of despondency at having witnessed so much Blood shed in vain; the blame rests somewhere, & our Brigade have been, & continue to be the victims of some shameful mismanagement; our Casualties continue very distressing. The Troops on the other side of the River appear to have done absolutely nothing, and the whole force of the Enemy has thus been permitted to fall upon us. To add·to our Misfortunes, the Weather yesterday set in very bad, and continues to-day a most threatening appearance. The Troops are so completely exhausted by hard labour, that should the Enemy make another vigorous Sortie, our Situation would be eminently critical.

15. To our utter astonishment an Order was received on the Afternoon of the 13th to suspend the Operations, & to convey to Elvas the various stores belonging to the Engineers, Artillery & Commissariat: at the same time we found a similar Order had been issued on the other Side of the Watër. This Order was said to be the consequence of the Marshal having received information that Soult was on full march to attack us with a superior force. Yesterday morning a dispatch arrived directing the Order of the preceding day to be suspended inasmuch as it was possible, & accordingly expresses were sent to Elvas to bring back the Stores. On the opposite Side, this Order could not be obeyed, as from the want of conveyance they had been obliged to burn a vast quantity; no directions were however given to continue the Operations. Everything continued the whole day in a state of uncertainty. This has however been relieved this morning by another Order, to send off without any delay all the Stores to Elvas, & in consequence every exertion is

(With the above words the writer's first notebook comes to its close. The narrative has evidently been at once carried on into a second book, of which the first leaf,

*containing some two hundred and sixty-five words has
unfortunately perished. The tale, as we have it, re-
commences in the middle of a sentence).*

possible at a Ford about a League above the town of Badajos;
the necessity was urgent as Soult with a large Army was
rapidly advancing upon Marshal Beresford; it was however
found impracticable, and at night we quitted our ground &
proceeded to Elvas. The following morning (16th) we
marched to Olivenza; the distance being five leagues, & the
roads dreadfully bad, it was near dark before we reached that
place. There we learned that an Engagement had that day
taken place, the result of which we could not that Night
collect. At One o'Clock the following Morning we proceeded
in the direction of Valverde, & from thence to Albouera, near
which place the Battle had been fought. On our arrival on
the Field of Combat a Scene the most horrible that the
imagination can conceive presented itself. The ground was
covered with the dead & the dying. It appeared that Soult
having collected a Force amounting to twenty five thousand
Men, of which number at least five thousand were Cavalry, &
relying upon his superiority in this latter Force in a Country
so favourable for their acting, in the confidence of success
resolved to attack the allied Army of British, Spanish, &
Portugueze, amounting to thirty thousand. The attack commenced on the morning of the 16th by a feint on the left, which
was immediately succeeded by the real attack on the right. The
Allies of both Nations fought bravely; but the British as
usual had the brunt of the Action; the Conflict between them
& the Enemy was dreadful. The battle did not terminate till
towards Evening, when they retired in every direction. The
loss of the allied Army is estimated at five thousand Men, of
which number at least four thousand were British. It is
supposed the Enemy suffered in a still greater proportion. It
is difficult to say on which side the Victory lay; we had the
honour of repulsing the Enemy in his attack, and frustrating

his intention of relieving Badajos; moreover all his wounded fell into our hands: on the other side, in a charge made by his Cavalry he succeeded in taking near a thousand of our Men Prisoners, besides the Colours of three Regiments and a Howitzer. Each Party will doubtless claim the Day, but the decision must be made by some who cannot be weighed in it by partiality. The Enemy retreated across a Plain, & took up his Position in a thick wood about two Miles from the Scene of Action; there he remained the whole of the following day.—It now became a general opinion that he would either retreat that Night, or attack us again the following Morning. At Daylight on the 18th we had the satisfaction of finding he had preferred the former. His Cavalry still shewed a front & some skirmishing took place; in the course of the forenoon they were entirely gone. This Movement was a great relief to every one; the British Troops had suffered so severely, that another Attack was anticipated with much apprehension; besides the wounded demanded the utmost care, & in the event of such another Day the loss of lives from the impossibility of giving proper attendance to all would have been very great indeed.—Yesterday (19th) our Brigade was employed in carrying wounded Men to Valverde. We encamped near that place last Night, & this Morning joined the Army. We have taken up our Position in the Wood occupied by the Enemy after the Action. It does not appear that they are rapidly retreating; their rear Guard is not more than four Leagues from hence. In the opinion of many they will return, & give us Battle again, it being an object of great importance to them to save Badajos. In the meantime our hopes are elated by the expectation of seeing Lord Wellington, who is to arrive this Evening. Two Divisions of the Army are likewise on their march here in order to oppose Reynier, who is advancing in this direction with his Corps; so that this is likely to become the chief scene of Action. For my own part I have been so completely horrified at the dreadful Scenes I have lately been compelled to witness, that they have given me a disgust for the Army I never before entertained. I see however no prospect of an early termination to the Campaign; on the contrary every thing seems to indicate that it will be a very protracted one. It is to be hoped we shall see but few more such Battles as that of the 16th, as they would in a very short time render the British Army a mere Name.

23d. We remained in the wood during the 21st, & marched from it Yesterday Morning at daybreak in the direction of Almandralejo. We halted for the Night about two Leagues from that place, understanding that the enemy continued in the neighbourhood of Azenchal. The Army moved forward this Morning in that direction, with the intention of giving them a broad hint to take themselves off; on arriving near we found they had gone. The 2d Division was therefore directed to march to Almandralejo into Cantonments, & our Division (the 4th) is quartered in Azenchal. We have now the expectation of remaining some Days quiet, and indeed the Army stands much in need of it. This is a miserable place for the accommodation of so many. The French quitted it yesterday Morning, which furnishes the Inhabitants with an excellent excuse for denying the possession of any one Comfort, alleging that they took away every thing away with them. It is melancholy to observe the Apathy that prevails among the People in general; it appears to me that they think it a matter of little moment whether they surrender their independence or not.

A letter from a Genl. Gazan to Soult has been intercepted in which he says that he has with him four thousand some hundred wounded in want of every species of Aid & Comfort; he mentions also having been obliged to leave three hundred in Almandralejo, which we have found to be the case. Their loss on the 16th was very great, it cannot be estimated at a less number than eight thousand. Lord Wellington has taken up his Head Quarters at Elvas and Badajos is again invested by a Division of Portugueze; there is no doubt that, when the Siege begins, it will be carried on with the utmost vigour; half measures do not suit his Lordship.

25th. We remain in Azenchal, nor have we any prospect of soon quitting it. Our accommodation is but bad, however it is luxury compared with what we have lately been accustomed to. We are in hopes of remaining here during the Siege. The 3rd & 7th Divisions have ere this arrived before Badajos, & they with the Portugueze will form an ample Force.

Our loss on the Battle of the 16th is as follows :—

	Killed	Wounded	Missing	Total
British	886	2705	547	4138
Portugueze	102	252	26	380
Total	988	2957	573	4518

221 Officers included in the above.

The Spaniards had 1500 Men killed & wounded &c. The only General Officer killed was Majr. Genl. Houghton; Majr. Genls. the Hon. W. Stewart & the Hon. G. L. Cole both commanding Divisions were wounded. The Army has particularly to lament the Death of Sir Wm. Myers, who fell at the head of the Fusilier Brigade which he was leading on most gallantly; at an early Age he had attained very high rank being a Lieut. Col. at Eighteen; his superior Abilities excessive zeal & entire devotion to the Service however proved that he was admirably qualified for the situation he filled; he died at the age of twenty eight, and his Death may be justly considered as a most severe loss to his Country.

By a distinguished act of gallantry a Corporal of Artillery prevented a Gun from falling into the Hands of the Enemy; Lord Wellington with a liberality worthy his great mind has given him an hundred Dollars, & directed him to be promoted on the first vacancy.

We have accounts of the fall of Almeida, which completes the entire expulsion of the Enemy from Portugal. So great a blessing the Portugueze as a Nation have deserved; their loyalty and devotedness to a sacred cause are unparallelled in the history of Nations, and do them immortal honour. Could I witness but a twentieth part of their loyalty in the Spaniards, I should anticipate their emancipation with Confidence. As it is I confess I look forward with more of fear than hope. They appear disposed to be content under any Government. Such a People deserve not to enjoy the sacred blessing of Freedom.

27th. A very brilliant affair took place on the 25tb between our heavy Dragoons and a portion of the Enemy's Cavalry. A small number of ours only showed themselves which induced the French to cross a narrow Bridge for the purpose of attacking them : the main Body then fell upon them, and routed them with great slaughter. Their loss in killed, wounded, & missing was four hundred besides many Officers : we had only three killed and twenty wounded.

We have no expectation of any thing being done for some time ; Marshal Beresford has quitted the Army for Elvas, from whence it is said he proceeds to Lisbon for the purpose of still further augmenting the Portugueze Force.—Genl. Hill is daily expected here to take the command of this Corps of the Army ; he is a very popular Officer.—The Marines & Artificers belonging to the Regiments in this Neighbourhood to be employed at the Siege of Badajos marched from hence this Morning.

30th. The Siege of Badajos has not yet commenced, but the preparations on a very large scale are going on as fast as possible. Lord W. has taken possession of a Quinta in the Neighbourhood, & his presence will infuse energy in every one concerned in the Operations. In the meantime Soult is collecting another Army at Llerena, which is only nine Leagues from here. He has at present a numerous Cavalry and about twelve thousand Infantry. It is supposed that Reynier with about ten thousand Men has reached Truxillo, and he will doubtless effect his junction with Soult. Unless the latter however can get further reinforcements from the South he will not be in strength to raise the Siege. The heat of the Weather is dreadful, and will I fear be productive of much Sickness in this Corps of the Army; indeed I think it probable notwithstanding the warlike appearance of every thing that in the course of the next six Months we shall lose more Men by Sickness than by the Sword.

[JUNE] June 2d. We hear nothing further of the Enemy, nor have we any reason to believe that they will be able to raise the Siege. We are in hopes that our Batteries opened this Morning, and, as they are on an immense scale, it is generally believed the place will fall in a few days. What are the intentions of Lord W. when this occurs we know not; it is generally thought however that we shall not advance far into the interior of this Country.

5th. We have reason to believe that the Batteries opened on the 3d. They are said to be excessively formidable, consisting of about fifty pieces of heavy Canon besides a large quantity of Mortars & Congreve Rockets. One of the Batteries was erected only fifty paces from the Walls. To prevent the Enemy from hearing the Men at Work during the Construction the following expedient was hit on :—several hundred Sheep & Goats each with a Bell about the neck were driven immediately under the walls between the intended Battery & the enemy; the noise they made effectually prevented the French from knowing what was going on till Daylight, by which time the work was completed. General Hill, who has been in England some time severely indisposed, arrived yesterday to take the Command of the two Divisions of the Army in this Neighbourhood; he is a Man of such conciliating manners & of a disposition so truly amiable that his return has excited the most lively satisfaction.

8th. It appears that the walls at Badajos are so excessively hard, that the progress in the Siege is by no means so quick as the Engineers had flattered themselves; no particular

Day is now mentioned when the Breach may be expected to be complete. It is said that Fort St. Christoval will be taken to-night by Storm ; the possession of it will materially contribute to the success of the ulterior Operations ; ·the excessive heat of the weather and the entire want of Shelter must make the whole duty most painful to the besiegers. We hear nothing further of the Enemy ; but it cannot be doubted that Soult is making every exertion to raise a Force sufficient to compel us to abandon our intentions.

10th. We yesterday received Orders to be in immediate readiness to march, which were repeated early this Morning with directions to have the Baggage Animals kept saddled ; eight hours have elapsed since this latter Order, & we hear no further on the subject.

An attempt was made the other Night upon St. Christoval, which failed, as is said, from the Storming Party mistaking the proper place and the Ladders being too short by several feet ; we lost fifty Men on the occasion.

11th. 10 a.m. We have this moment received orders to march and to reach Albouera this Evening. There is not a doubt that the enemy are in motion, and it seems probable there will be another sanguinary Contest on the same ground; much depends upon the issue.

Another unsuccessful attempt was made upon St. Christoval the Night before last : we lost many Men ; it is said that the Siege was raised last night.

13th. We quitted Azenchal on the Afternoon of the 11th, but did not march further than a League ; we are encamped in an Olive Grove midway between Azenchal & Solano on the Road leading to Albouera. Every thing is again quiet in front, the movements of the Enemy the other day could have been nothing more than a reconnoissance, tho' it is highly probable they will again advance. It seems certain that the Siege of Badajos has been converted into a Blockade ; the

Engineers found too late that they had erected their breaching Batteries against the most impregnable part of the place ; they were literally battering a Rock.   Much Blood has been most unsuccessfully spilt.   Our hopes now rest on being able to keep Soult in check and starving the Garrison ; this is at the best uncertain.   No blame is imputed to Lord W. ; there is no doubt that he was deceived by the too sanguine representations of the Engineers.

15th.   We marched at noon on the 13th from our encampment near Solano, and proceeded two Leagues in the direction of Albouera, when we halted ; at two o'Clock in the Morning of yesterday we again marched, & encamped in the wood occupied by the Enemy after the Battle of the 16th, & in which we halted after they quitted it ; there is no doubt that Lord Wellington has selected the same Position for the Scene of Action.   His Head Quarters are in the Village of Albouera.   We do not exactly know where the Enemy's advance at present is ; but they continue approaching us, and it is probable that the conflict will take place in a day or two.

16th.   It is supposed that Marshal Marmont who lately succeeded Massena in the command of the French Northern Army is advancing rapidly on the right bank of the Guadiana. When joined with Soult, they would have such an alarming superiority, that it would be rashness, if not madness, to think of engaging them.   In consequence we last Evening quitted the wood, and crossing the river at the bridge of Albouera remained for the Night on some heights above that place ; at 3 o'clock this morning we marched in the direction of Badajos, & are now halted in a wood about a League from that Town. Our sojourn here is very precarious, having just received Orders to have every thing prepared to start again at a Moment's Notice.   Of the intentions of his Lordship we are ignorant, but it is generally conceived we are going to the other side of the Guadiana for the purpose of taking up some strong position till we can be joined by Genl. Spencer, who is said to be advancing with our Northern Army. This necessity is to be lamented as it compels us to uncover Badajos, and thus defeats at once what we have spilt so much valuable blood in endeavouring to attain.

19th. On the 17th we quitted our encampment near Badajos, and crossing the Guadiana at a Ford halted in an Olive Grove in the Vicinity of Elvas. The Day turned out most severe, and during the Night the Thunder & Lightning were truly awful, no Person in the Camp ever having experienced anything so dreadfully terrific; the Rain came down in such Torrents, that in a very short time we were almost completely under water. In Consequence Yesterday Morning we were ordered into Elvas, which place we quitted again this Day; we are at present halted about two Leagues on the Road leading to Portalegre, and, as we suppose, in the neighbourhood of our Position, provided the French choose to attack us in it. They have an immense Force, Marmont having certainly united with Soult. To counteract this General Spencer with the principal part of our Northern Army has made a parallel movement, and can join us in a few hours. The desponding are of opinion that we shall be immediately compelled to retire to our Lines, whereas others think that the combined movement of the Enemy was merely for the purpose of throwing in succours into Badajos; having effected which they will cease to molest us. Lord W. has however prepared for the worst; under the possibility that Elvas may be besieged, the Inhabitants have been recommended to quit their Houses, and every other necessary precaution has been made.

There is a report very current & which has gained some credit at Head Quarters viz., that we have taken in the Mediterranean ten Sail of the Line, having nine thousand Troops on board, making a push from Toulon to Catalonia, where it is certain the Enemy have lately been losing ground. Should this prove true, it will very materially alter the nature of things in the Peninsula, and Soult will most assuredly be obliged to retrace his steps hastily.

23d. We still continue in the same encampment, tho' our stay in it is very uncertain. Yesterday was a day of bustle; the Enemy kept us constantly on the qui vive; they shewed themselves in considerable force both in the Neighbourhood of Elvas & Campo Mayor. In a skirmish we took two Officers and some Men, but most unfortunately a Picquet of the 11th Dragoons, just arrived from England, was surprised, & three Officers & forty Men made Prisoners; the enemy retired to Badajos in the afternoon, and they have not since been seen. Opinions are divided whether this movement was a reconnoisance previous to their advancing, or if it was only intended to cover a retrograde Movement towards Seville, they having succeeded in their object of throwing succours into Badajos.

28th. A severe pectoral complaint compelled me to quit the Regiment on the 23d for the purpose of avoiding the night dews. I was recommended to try the air of Portalegre, at which place I arrived the 24th, and still remain, having found the greatest benefit from the few Days I have been here. Portalegre is generally considered the Montpellier of Portugal; it is prettily situated surrounded by Hills chiefly covered with the Olive; like the other large Towns in this Country it abounds with Priests of every description. I had an opportunity this day of seeing the Bishop officiate in the Cathedral, and I must say a more undignified Gentleman I never saw; very unlike indeed my good Friend, the Bishop of Guarda.

This place is seven Leagues from the Head Quarters of the Army. I have no certain accounts from thence, but it appears that the Enemy having gained their object of relieving Badajos have again retired, and, as it is said, in two Columns, one on Merida, & the other in the direction of Seville, for the purpose of preventing Blake (who marched some days since with the whole Spanish force) from getting possession of that place.

English papers to the 12th instant inform us that the good people there are highly delighted with the battle of Albouera, and it even appears that two great Houses have unanimously decreed their thanks to a certain Individual " for the distinguished ability displayed by him &c. &c." O Tempora, O Mores.

July 3d. It having been satisfactorily ascertained that the Enemy had retired, the Army Yesterday marched into Cantonments ; the 5th Division entered this place (Portalegre). Having again in great measure regained my wonted health, I purpose going to-morrow in search of my Regt.

Great reinforcements are expected from England ; but it is hoped that nothing will be done till the three next months shall have passed by, as the extreme heat in this Country in the Months of July, August, and September occasions even under Circumstances the most favourable great degree of sickness amongst the Troops.

9th. Only three Divisions of the Army are in Cantonments, the uncertainty of the Enemy's Movements rendering it necessary that the remainder should be accessible to act as circumstances may require. I found my Division in the same place I left it. It does not seem likely that anything will be done for some time. It is said the Enemy are concentrating everything in Estremadura, and in the meantime reinforcements are daily arriving from England ; probably, when the hot season is over, a great blow may be struck.

Genl. Graham, the Conqueror at Barrosa, is coming here as second in command. This appointment has given universal satisfaction ; the various Casualties of war might possibly deprive us of the Services of Lord W., and under such a calamity it would be a great consolation to every one that the Command of the Army should devolve on an Officer of such avowed talents as Genl. Graham.

14. Nothing whatever in the shape of news has lately occurred. Reinforcements continue to arrive from England,

and amongst others four hundred men & upwards have arrived to join my Regiment; this puts out of all probability the likelihood of our returning to England, even tho' circumstances should eventually oblige us to quit the Peninsula; which however appears less probable than ever.

25th. On the 21st we broke up from our encampment, and marched in the direction of Elvas, near which place we remained for the night. The 22nd we continued our route, & bivouacked in the Neighbourhood of Borba. The following morning we reached Estremos, where we are likely to remain some time, it being destined as the Quarters of the 4th Division. The whole Army are now in Cantonments, & it is expected they will remain so during the continuance of the hot Season, which lasts till about the first week in October. On leaving our encampment strict Orders were issued not on any account to destroy the huts, from whence is inferred the possibility that we may have at some future time to occupy them again. Head quarters are at Portalegre & the different Cantonments of the Army extend from the Tagus to the Guadiana.

30th. The old Adage of their being nothing certain under the Sun is at present abundantly verified by our receiving orders to quit our cantonments, & march to-morrow Morning in the direction of Castello Branco. This has come most unexpectedly upon us, as everyone was making himself comfortable at least for a period of two months. It appears that Tarragona has fallen, & that Soult is marching upon Carthagena; Marmont is in consequence left alone, and it is supposed Lord W. is going to attack him before he can be reinforced.

[AUG.] August 4. We marched from Estremos according to route on the 31st, & bivouacked near the small Town of Fronteira. On the 1st we proceeded to Crato, four Leagues further, where we were miserably accommodated in Cantonments. On the 2nd we marched to Alpalhão two Leagues, &

yesterday arrived at Nisa, two more Leagues, where we halt this Day.

We are still entirely in the dark as to the cause of our present movement. Many are of opinion that Lord W. is about to make a demonstration on Madrid, in order to compel the Enemy in the South to desist from their operations there. It appears more probable however that we are going into Cantonments in the North; there is no doubt that a vast number of lives will be saved by such a change of Quarters.

We continue our march to-morrow Morning, and shall cross the Tagus at Villa Velha for the purpose of proceeding to Castel Branco, where we shall receive another Route.

8th. On the 5th we quitted Nisa, & marched by almost impassable Roads to Villa Velha, three Leagues ; the following Day we proceeded to a small village called Sarnadas, and yesterday morning reached the ancient City of Castel Branco. It is a Bishop's See, but the Cathedral & Town are alike in a state of great dilapidation. The Palace and Gardens of his Reverence however are in complete repair, and have an Air of luxury and Comfort about them I have not before witnessed in this Country.

When we reached Castel Branco, the General Officer Comg. the Division was without Orders to proceed any further. In the course of the Day however an Order was received directing us to march this Morning towards Penamacor, which, tho' only eight Leagues distant from Castel Branco, we are to be four Days in performing. The excessive heat of the Weather renders it impossible to go long marches without infinite injury to the Troops ; a great deal of sickness at present prevails, to which a number of officers are victims; indeed I consider the Climate of this Country during the hot months in Autumn as little less unhealthy than the West Indies.

No enquiries we could make have been able to give us the smallest insight into the intentions of Lord Wellington.

Every one therefore is at perfect liberty to enjoy his own Opinion, and we wait till Time shall disclose whose Speculation is the wisest.

13th. On the 9th we marched to San Miguel, two Leagues, and on the 10th to Pedrogo, the same distance. At the latter place we were to go into Villages in the Neighbourhood ; accordingly on the morning of the 11th the Division went into its several Cantonments. Our Regiment is in two wretched Villages, merely affording Covering ; we can purchase no one Article whatever. It is probable we shall not remain here many days. The Divisions in our front are said to be moving, & we hear that our advance is within three leagues of Ciudad Rodrigo. Among other Speculations many are of opinion that Lord W. is about to attack that Fortress to prevent his left flank from being constantly menaced ; the idea is at least plausible, tho' there may be no intention whatever to undertake such an Operation.

The name of our principal Village is Aldea de João Perez, about a League from Penamacor.

17. We hear nothing about moving, but it appears that the Enemy were at a Village about five Leagues from hence the day before yesterday demanding Rations ; it is not supposed they are coming in this direction, but that they are moving in the direction of Ciudad Rodrigo, which place it is asserted Lord W. is certainly threatening. Head Quarters are beyond the Frontier, but I know not at what place.

20. The enemy continue to make their occasional appearance within a few Leagues of us. Two or three Days since they took a Convoy of Mules laden with Provisions for the Light Division ; a party of the 16th Dragoons, and an officer were also surprized. It is certain that our Cavalry are by no means so expert in the Out Post duty as the German Hussars ; there is no instance of their having been surprized.

24. We are likely to remain in this wretched place a considerable time; the Weather is dreadfully hot, but the Troops are much healthier than they were a week ago.

Reinforcements, particularly Dragoons, continue to arrive from England, and Lord W. in the last Gazette appears as a General with temporary Rank, that is, in Spain & Portugal only. The papers to the 7th inst. give a deplorable acct. of His Majesty's state ; indeed they leave little reason to hope that he is now alive. On the accession of the Prince to the Throne, it is probable the same System with regard to this Country will be persevered in ; and, as the enemy themselves no longer talk of driving us into the sea, it is impossible to calculate when hostilities in the Peninsula will have an end.

29. On the evening of the 27th we received a sudden and most unexpected Order to commence our March in the direction of Penamacor, which place we passed through Yesterday Morning and halted near a village called Merimoa. This Day we have had a march of two long Leagues thro' a deplorably barren country. We are in bivouac in the neighbourhood of the wretched remains of a Village called San Antonio. Tomorrow we proceed Northward ; our destination is said to be in front of Almeida beyond the Frontier. It seems certain that Lord W. is about to commence the siege of Ciudad Rodrigo. The heavy battering Train will very soon be ready. From the circumstance of nearly the whole Army being brought up it is inferred that his Lordship will give battle to any Force the Enemy can bring to oppose him.

31. Our Route was Yesterday Morning changed, and we were directed to march to Villa de Toro, where we were to receive instructions as to the Cantonments we were this day to occupy. Accordingly at an early hour this morning the Division marched into different Villages, extending nearly in a line about three Leagues distant from Guarda. Here it was intended we should have remained for some time, but an Order has just arrived, directing us to march to-morrow & take up

our original destination, which we suppose to be between the Coa & the Agueda. We are entirely ignorant as to the cause of these different changes.

It was a twelvemonth yesterday since we quitted Guarda under circumstances which would have rendered the idea of our being at this time in the neighbourhood as nothing less than madness; there is no calculating on the future, but certainly during no period of the Contest have our prospects been brighter than at present.

[SEPT.] Sept. 2. We yesterday Morning marched from Mamolina to a village called Preixal. This Morning we proceeded to a village, whose Misery beggars description, & which unfortunately is assigned as our Cantonment; it is called San Pedro, & being only two Miles from the Spanish Frontier in the direction of Ciudad Rodrigo it has consequently frequently been visited by the Enemy, who have left it nearly a heap of Ruins.

5th. We hear nothing of the Enemy, nor are we as yet able to assign any probable cause for our movement to this part of the Country. Since I have been here I have had an opportunity of riding over to Almeida, it being only a league from hence and a most melancholy spectacle it presents; nothing can be more complete than the destruction of the Bastions; indeed with the exception of two or three houses the Town is one heap of undistinguished Ruins. I had also yesterday an opportunity of seeing Fort Conception, which is situated just within the Spanish Frontier; it was destroyed last year by order of Lord W. when the enemy advanced upon Almeida; its destruction also is very complete.

11th. It is reported that the Enemy are concentrating their Forces for the purpose of throwing succours into Ciudad Rodrigo, which are there much wanted; this Lord W. will of course endeavour to prevent unless he is greatly outnumbered. The Light Division are some distance in front of Ciudad Rodrigo in the direction of Salamanca. Sickness unhappily prevails to a melancholy extent in our Army; in my Regiment alone the present returns of Sick are fifteen Officers and six hundred Men. As the weather however is beginning to get cool, we are in hopes that the Troops will be more healthy; the total Amount of ineffectives at present is, I believe, not less than twenty thousand Men.

19th. Early on the Morning of the 17th our Division received a sudden Order to change its Cantonments; we marched four Leagues that Day, & bivouacked for the Night in the neighbourhood of a small village called Alamandilla; it is in Spain but chiefly inhabited by Portugueze. Yesterday morning we resumed our march, and reached our cantonment at the most wretched of all wretched Villages called Fencalhos : it is in Portugal; the remainder of the Division are in Spain. This is the second time we have had the ill luck to get into Portugueze Villages, when we expected to be in Spain : besides that the Enemy have not done a hundredth part of the mischief to the latter that they have to the former, there is an air of cleanliness in the Spanish Villages one can never meet with in Portugal, which renders the former so infinitely preferable as a Cantonment.

We know not whether anything is likely to be done soon or not. It is said the Great Convoy is expected to quit Salamanca as to-morrow. I should rejoice at anything that would remove us from the state of misery we are in in this place. We have observed every night for the last week a Comet from which is reflected a very considerable light; it is situated immediately under the Constellation of the Great Bear ; our being in this place is by many jocosely attributed to its malign influence.

21. There is a probability that we shall not remain long in this village: an Order has been received from Head Quarters for the Division to hold itself in readiness to march at a Moment's Notice. Whether our Movements will be forward or retrograde we have no idea ; it seems however that

the Enemy has been carrying everything before them in the South East of Spain, which may possibly frustrate the execution of any plans Lord Wellington contemplated in this quarter; should we be obliged to fall back it is thought we can take up a position on the Coa sufficiently strong to oppose any Force the Enemy can bring against us.

24th. We left Fencalhos yesterday Morng., & marched two Miles in front of Lord W's Head Quarters (Fuente de Guinaldo) where we are bivouacked. It is said that the enemy are in such force, that it was impossible to prevent them throwing Succours into Ciudad Rodrigo, which it is supposed entered that place Yesterday & this Morning : they are reported to be sixty thousand strong, which outnumbers us by at least fifteen Thousand. Tho' Lord W. does not feel himself strong enough to act offensively, it would appear that he thinks himself equal to defend himself if attacked; should they advance, the Contest will probably be in this Neighbourhood ; strong parties are at work throwing up entrenchments etc.

We are in Spain almost immediately on the banks of the Agueda (which washes the walls of Ciudad Rodrigo) and about four Leagues from that place.

29. On the 25th the Enemy in Force attacked the Division who were in advance beyond the Agueda. We were in consequence ordered to their support, but did not come into action as the affair was over before we came up. In the Evening both Divisions took up a Position in front of Fuente Guinaldo having the Enemy about three Miles from us in great Force. We fully expected to be attacked the next morning at Daylight & Lord W. had ordered every species of Baggage to be out of the Village an hour before daybreak ; they did not however come on. We remained the whole day in the same position, and from a height in our possession had a distinct view of the French Army, which was vastly superior to what we had supposed, amounting to about six thousand Cavalry and thirty thousand Infantry; whereas our Force

opposed to them was not more than fifteen hundred of the former and about twelve thousand of the latter. In the course of the Day further reinforcements were observed to come to them, as also a large Force of Artillery of the largest calibre. They had now such an overwhelming superiority that Lord W. directed the whole Army to retreat that night in the direction of Sabugal. The next morning (27th) a considerable part of our Force was assembled near a Village called Aldea de Ponte in Portugal, & about three Leagues distant from Fuente Guinaldo; at ten o'Clock the enemy's Cavalry began to appear, and in a very short time presented a most formidable appearance supported by Infantry; at noon they drove in our out posts and advanced rapidly upon us; the business lasted about an hour, when they were completely repulsed. All remained quiet for some hours, & we were about to make ourselves comfortable for the Night, when just before dusk they renewed their attack, and were repulsed, as in the Day. Our loss amounted in both affairs to not more than sixty in killed & wounded besides several Officers.—At two o'Clock Yesterday Morning we again commenced our march and halted at a place called Soito at Daylight; a position was taken up on some heights above it, and we were in a momentary expectation of again seeing the Enemy. They have not however since appeared, and without knowing anything certain an idea is entertained that they have taken the direction of Almeida by way of proceeding to Celorico, where we have Stores, a General Hospital &c. This idea is strengthened by the Circumstance of the 5th Division having received orders this morning (29th) to make a forced March beyond Sabugal in the direction of Guarda. We occupy still the high ground above Soito, but are in momentary expectation of an Order to march. It is not probable that the Enemy can with any force penetrate far into Portugal, as the Country is so entirely destitute of every species of supply; for my own part I conceive the game in Spain as nearly up, & I doubt not that our future attention will be almost exclusively directed to this

Country, which is as much as our limited means will enable us to defend.

Octr. 1.—Yesterday morning the Division received orders to march in the direction of the Coa for the purpose of being cantoned in Villages near it, but on this side of the River: as a temporary arrangement for the night we occupied a small place called Bismula, where we still remain. It was intended to have made the final arrangements this Morning, but during the Night, Orders were received from Lord W. for our Division to proceed to-morrow and occupy Villages about two Leagues in front of this, where it is probable we shall remain some time unless prevented by the Enemy. We shall have the Light Division on our right, but nothing in our front; we shall therefore be obliged to remain constantly on the alert & exposed to perpetual Alarms.

It is considered a most fortunate circumstance that we retreated from Fuente Guinaldo at the time we did. An Aid du Camp of Lord W.'s who went in with a Flag of Truce on the Morning of the 26th & was detained by them, but has since been sent in, states that they had a most overwhelming force, with which they meant to have attacked us the following Morning; while their Cavalry & Sharp shooters manoeuvred in our front, our right & left were to have been turned by twenty thousand Men on each flank. Our vast inferiority would have rendered it impossible to have sustained such an attack, and the consequences of a defeat under such circumstances would have been dreadful; in all probability Portugal would have been lost by it. It is scarcely to be wondered that Marmont was much annoyed when he found that Lord W. had eluded his plans, & he exclaimed " Voila encore la belle etoile de Wellington." Our incapacity to resist the enemy on this occasion arose from the absolute necessity Lord W. was under of watching the different entrances into Portugal, by which means it was impossible for him to concentrate a large force on any one point.—It appears that at the time we

commenced our march on the Morning of the 28th from above
Aldea de Ponte, expecting that the Enemy would follow us to
the Position near Soito, where Lord W. was determined to give
them Battle, & under circumstances that promised the most
happy issue, they had themselves gone off two hours before
quite satisfied with the reception they had met with in their
two attacks on the preceding day ; they returned thro' Fuente
Guinaldo with Colours flying, Bands playing etc. etc. assuring
the Inhabitants that they had near annihilated the British
Army.

It is pleasing to observe the decided antipathy to French
dominion that still pervades the Breasts of the Portugueze.
When we commenced our retreat the other Evening, & the
poor People were of course ignorant how far we might go,
they one and all packed up what little they had, & with the
utmost cheerfulness set off as last year for the Mountains.
Whilst this Spirit continues amongst them, it is impossible
they can be subdued.

5th. The 4th Division is cantoned in Villages extending
from Villa Formosa to Nava d'Aver, at which latter place we
are quartered ; Almeida & Fuente d'Onore likewise are a part
of the Cantonments of our Division ; Genl. Crawford with the
Light Division occupies different villages on our right ; the
Head Quarters of the Army are at Frenada, about a League
in our rear. There is no doubt that the French have all left
this Neighbourhood, but it is not yet satisfactorily
ascertained, whether the whole body has retired from Salamanca, or whether a large portion of them have taken the
route towards Gallicia for the purpose of destroying the
Spanish Army at present organising there.

The 97th Regiment, being almost entirely wasted by the
casualties of war, marched thro' this place yesterday on their
way to Lisbon to embark for England. It is impossible to
conceive a more happy set of Fellows than they appeared ; as
they marched by, they excited certain emotions in my Mind,

which can only be conceived by those who have experienced a long and painful exile from a beloved Country.

We are not in expectation of having anything to do for several Months, but the idea is that the Enemy will make every effort to concentrate such an overwhelming force by the ensuing Spring, as shall render all resistance on our part unavailing. Unquestionably the majority of the Officers of this Army would hail any Circumstance that should compel us to quit the Peninsula without absolute disgrace ; nor indeed can it be wondered at, for the History of all former Wars furnishes no parallel to the sufferings and privations endured both by the Officers & Soldiers in Spain and Portugal. I trust however that such will not be the case, but that the gallantry and constancy of this People will ultimately be rewarded by the entire expulsion of the Enemy.

This place is not less miserable than those we have lately occupied ; in wet weather the very best houses are absolutely incapable of affording protection ; the Equinoctials which have now set in find access by a thousand different entrances. We are four Leagues from Ciudad Rodrigo.

8th. We have not a word of the Enemy, and the probability of there being nothing done for some time to come may be considered fortunate for us, as the Army was never before in such a state of inefficiency ; the Sick in our Regiment alone amount to seven hundred & fifty, being exactly one half ; the prevailing disease is Intermittent Fever, which, tho' not so violent, is scarcely less prevalent than the Walcheren Ague.

The Comet is still visible, & in greater brilliancy than ever ; it has changed its situation, being at present over the Tail of the Constellation of the Great Bear, instead of under it, as it first appeared.

It seems that the affair of the 25th Ulto. was one of the most gallant that has taken place in this Country. Lord W.

has expressed his sense of it in terms of approbation quite unusual to him. He was himself in the whole of it, and had thus an opportunity of observing the gallantry he so much admired. It is nothing less than miraculous how he escapes on these occasions, as he constantly exposes himself in the most unguarded manner; his Staff both on that day & the 27th were in utmost alarm for his safety. The Regiments who distinguished themselves on the 25th were the 1st German Hussars & 11th Dragoons, and the 2nd Battn. 5th & 77th Regiments, and 21st Regt. of Portugueze Infantry.

13th. The Enemy are in considerable force at Placentia, and it is conjectured that they will unite with the Army of the South, and endeavour to make an irruption into the Alemtejo. Should this be the case, we shall of course be compelled to retrace the steps we so lately trod, and make the best of our way to that part of the Country. The weather is at present fine, but, as the wet season may be almost immediately expected, we anticipate a march of such magnitude with no very agreeable feelings.

Lord W.'s dispatch to the Regency states that the Force we should have had opposed to us at Guinaldo, had we waited their attack, was not less than Sixty thousand, among which were six thousand Cavalry & twenty two Battalions of the Imperial Guards; their Artillery amounted to one hundred and twenty five pieces. When reflecting on the small force we had to oppose to this terrific one, it is impossible to contemplate without horror the consequences that might have resulted, had we awaited the result of so unequal a conflict.

17th. Our Division yesterday changed its cantonments; we now occupy a line extending from Espeja on the right to Barba del Puerco on the left; the 40th are quartered in Gallegos, distant only eight Miles from Ciudad Rodrigo. The Enemy's Garrison there consists of a few Cavalry, and about two thousand five hundred Infantry; we are not therefore very apprehensive of a visit from them; such a proceeding would be extremely hazardous. A Party of Don Julian's Men succeeded the day before yesterday in taking the Governor & several other Officers Prisoners : they were on a riding excursion in the Vicinity of the place, when these people surprized them. They likewise took two hundred & sixty head of Cattle, besides Sheep and Goats ; this loss will doubtless be very seriously felt by them.

26th. There was an idea Yesterday Evening that the Enemy meditated an attack upon San Felices de Chico last night for the purpose of possessing himself of a considerable quantity of Bullocks that are in the vicinity of that place ; we were in consequence ordered to keep on the alert, and the Men were directed to sleep accoutred ; no alarm however took place.

Nothing can possibly exceed the dullness and monotony of our present mode of life. We know nothing whatever of the enemy, but it is certain that they have no other force near us than the Garrison of Ciudad Rodrigo.

[Nov.]   Novr 3d. Information was received two or three Days ago that the Enemy were again concentrating a Force, with the object, as was supposed, of throwing in more Stores & particularly Bullocks into Ciudad Rodrigo, in lieu of those taken from them lately by Don Julian. In consequence, the Night before last we were ordered to proceed as yesterday Morning at daylight & unite with the Light Division at El Bodon, a Village about four Leagues on our right, and two from Ciudad Rodrigo, from whence we were to have gone to another Village called Pastores with the intention of intercepting the Convoy. On our arrival at El Bodon we found that we were one day too late, as the Enemy had thrown in the supplies and a new Governor at eight o'Clock the preceding Night, and after resting a few hours the escort, consisting of about five thousand men, had again quitted the place. In this instance Lord W's information was very incorrect ; had we been twenty four hours sooner something very dashing might have been done. We were directed (as were the whole Army) to return to our Cantonments, which we did this day.

Circumstances have turned out much more favourably in the South under General Hill; we have not all the particulars, but it appears that ten days ago, Genl. H. surprized a Corps of the enemy under Genl. Girard, and besides killing a great many made a thousand Prisoners & took three pieces of Cannon. The Prince of D'Aremberg & Genl. Brunn were also taken as was Genl. Girard, but the latter got away afterwards. The Duke D'Aremberg, brother to the Prince, was among the killed. The brilliancy of this affair is considerably enhanced by its having been performed almost without bloodshed, our loss on the occasion being only thirty in killed & wounded. We may expect to hear of many more Prisoners being made, as, when the despatches came away, the Cavalry were in pursuit, & the Enemy's force were in the utmost disorder & completely dispersed.—General Hill is a man so entirely beloved by every one, that the business having been atchieved by him has afforded the most general and lively satisfaction.

On our way to and from El Bodon, we passed over the hill on which was placed the Portugueze Artillery on the 25th Sept. It was taken by the enemy and retaken by a most gallant and successful charge made by the 5th Regiment. The scene of action is marked by the unburied Bones of the unfortunate French, who on that day closed there their earthly career, victims of the Ambition of the wretch who is yet permitted by Heaven to live as a scourge to Europe.

15th. Since my last date no single circumstance whatever has occurred worth relating; at Head Quarters Chimnies are building in all the Houses, and everything appears to indicate a long period of inactivity. Lord W. has got out a pack of Fox Hounds from England, with which he amuses himself twice a week; several Accidents have occurred from severe falls, and amongst others the Prince of Orange narrowly escaped with his life.

We are now a period of fifty two Days without News from England, the longest time since the British Army have been in the Peninsula; the wind having got Northerly we are anxiously expecting the Mail, when we shall be inundated with Papers; by them we shall have, it is probable, the investment of the Prince with the full powers of Royalty, and also we may expect some insight into his intentions and policy respecting these countries.

[DEC.] Decr. 1. On the 23d Ulto. an order was received to march immediately in the direction of El Bodon. We halted for the day at a small Village called Arrapiles, and resumed our march the following Morning for El Bodon. On our arrival there we found there was not room for us, & we were directed to retrograde to Fuente Guinaldo. The whole Army was in motion, and it was generally understood that a large Convoy with a very strong escort, was on its way from Salamanca to Ciudad Rodrigo. We remained at Guinaldo till the 29th, when we were ordered to resume our former Cantonments. The Divisions that had been a considerable way in the rear, have fresh Cantonments assigned them, more to the front. It does not appear certain whether another convoy was on its way, or whether the large body of French Troops from Salamanca that moved in the direction of Ciudad Rodrigo was not a party intended to levy Contributions on all the intermediate Towns. It seems that Lord Wellington expects something will yet be done, as each Regiment has orders to make itself thoroughly acquainted with all the Roads in our Front. The weather is fine but excessively cold and frosty. Our Regiment is still very ineffective from sickness; the convalescence is very protracted, & the relapses are frequent; indeed the Corps has this Autumn received a shock it will, I fear, be a very long time recovering.

Our last accounts from England inform us that Parliament is further postponed. The policy of the Regent therefore as far as regards the Peninsula remains yet to be discovered. It would seem almost impossible that the enormous expense attending this contest can be long supported; Money is already so scarce that the Army is only paid up to the 24th August, an arrear unprecedented in our Military History; the supplies also in consequence are not so good as formerly; a plenty might be obtained, but the People are tired of promissory payment, & conceal their Corn, etc, etc.

11th. It is rumoured that the enemy purpose attempting to introduce another convoy about the 20th, in the event of which it is supposed we shall cross the Agueda at a Ford in our front (if the Rains do not set in very much) instead of going round by El Bodon. It is certain, notwithstanding Marmont's boast of having thrown in supplies for a year, that they are by no means well off for Provisions ; it will however be impossible for them to relieve the place, unless they bring a Force superior to ours, which at this Season of the year they cannot do without the utmost annoyance to themselves.

The Affairs in the Peninsula fluctuate between hope & fear. The Enemy as a prelude to the conquest at Valencia, have taken the Fortress of Sagunto. They obtained it by Capitulation after five ineffectual attempts to take it by Storm. On the other hand, the Guerillas are daily increasing in numbers & boldness. A most brilliant affair was lately performed by the celebrated Partizan Mina ; with nine hundred men he attacked eleven hundred of the enemy of which number three only escaped who were not either killed or made Prisoners.

A singular hoax was a few days since played off upon the good People of Lisbon. Advertisements were stuck up in all parts of the Town, stating that a British Officer had invented a pair of Cork Boots of a very singular construction, with which he purposed on such a day at twelve o'Clock to walk across the Tagus from Belem to the opposite side of the River and to return at one. Almost the whole Population of Lisbon repaired to Belem to witness this extraordinary feat: the Tower was reserved for the Regency, Marshall Beresford and the other great characters with their Families; it exhibited a Blaze if not of Beauty, at least of Diamonds. After waiting several hours, and no performer appearing, they perceived the hoax, & departed to their respective homes, each laughing at the other.

28. Nothing particular has occurred since the last date. We hear nothing of any intention on the part of the Enemy to throw further supplies into Ciudad Rodrigo. The successes of the Spaniards in the South have obliged Marmont to detach a portion of his Army to reinforce Suchet in Valencia. In the meantime Lord Wellington is building a Bridge on the Agueda, which is already in a considerable state of forwardness. The Engineer Department have orders to provide every requisite for an immediate Siege. Some think that Lord W. taking advantage of Marmont's present weakness will certainly attack Ciudad Rodrigo, notwithstanding the unfavourable Season of the Year; while others are of opinion the great preparations making are nothing more than a demonstration, to compel the French Chief to recall the Detachments he has sent to the South. It is devoutly to be wished that the latter may be the real object, as from the severity of the Weather and the generally exhausted state of the Army the consequences of taking the Field must be dreadful.

[1812]
[JAN.]

Jan. 4. There is too much reason to fear that we shall take the Field in the course of a very few days, notwithstanding the weather is at present as bad as it can possibly be.

We march to-morrow Morning to San Felices El Chico, a small village to our left, for the purpose of making room for Head Quarters and the Guards who come here. This place is a scene of the utmost hurry and bustle; nothing to be seen but Engineers, & all the Implements requisite for a Siege; the Bridge will be completed the day after to-morrow.

Doubtless Lord W. must have some extraordinary and most urgent reasons for commencing the Siege at this inclement season. The consequences to the health of the Army I shudder to think of, it is scarcely too much to expect that every one who has suffered from disease during the last six months will not relapse. Should this be the case, the Troops will be absolutely inefficient to any active operations in the Spring. Every one appears astonished, and all contemplate the preparations with a horror equal to their wonder.

5. The order for our March this day was last Night countermanded ; but it is feared that it is only a suspension for twenty four hours in consequence of the Bridge not being quite ready.

12. We did not leave Gallegos till the 7th, when we came to a small Village called Villa de Porco, where we still remain ; on the 8th Ciudad Rodrigo was invested, & the Evening of the same day a Redoubt of considerable importance to the final success of the enterprise was attacked and carried in very fine style by a Party of the Light Division under the orders of Col. Colburne of the 52d Regt. On the same Night ground was broke ; the Siege is carried on each Day by a Division of the Army ; the Light, 1st 3d & 4th are the whole employed. We took the duty on the 10th. During the twenty four hours our casualties amounted to three killed & twelve wounded, which was more than a half of the loss of the whole Division. There appeared much despondency at the commencement of the business on the part of the Engineers, though they seem since to think better of it ; it is however rumoured that Marmont is assembling a formidable force, and many are of opinion he may succeed in raising the Siege. Our Batteries will not be ready to open these two or three Days. I have not heard what time it is calculated it will take to make a practicable breach, but it is certain that the Battering Train is as fine a one as ever was employed.—The weather is extremely cold, but very fine ; our Cantonment is twelve miles from Ciudad Rodrigo.—

There can be no doubt that Lord W. will give the Enemy Battle, unless the Enemy have a very superior force. Our three remaining Divisions are moving up from the rear. From the weakness of the Garrison in Ciudad one Brigade will be sufficient to keep it in check.

21. On the 13th the Convent of Saint Antonio was taken by a party of the German Legion ; it is situated near the River on our right & annoyed our workmen considerably. The following day our Division went again on duty, & the same Evening the 40th were directed to storm the Convent of San· Francisco, where the Enemy had a Mortar and Gun, which altogether prevented our going on with our Approaches. Considerable resistance was expected, but, on the Men appearing on the walls of the Convent, the Enemy fired a Volley, and fled to the Town with precipitation ; only three Men were wounded in this affair. We (the 40th) remained in possession of the Convent and Suburbs during the remainder of the Siege, instead of returning to our Cantonments, as was the case with the remainder of the Army. On the afternoon of the 14th our Batteries opened. On the 15th our fire was resumed with much spirit, and with considerable effect. On the 16th there was so impenetrable a fog, that scarcely a shot could be fired ; a new Battery however was nearly completed for the purpose of making a second breach ; on the Evening of the same day Lord W. summoned the Town, which was answered by the Governor in terms expressing his determination to perish in the Ruins rather than surrender. The 17th proving a beautiful Morning, our Batteries opened with great vivacity, and continued firing till Evening, at which time considerable progress was made in effecting the Breach. On the 18th the new Battery commenced ; by sunset the first Breach was declared practicable and much impression was made on the wall by the New Battery. At Noon on the 19th both Breaches were declared by the Engineers practicable, and every arrangement was made in consequence to storm the

Town the same Evening. For this duty, the Light and 3d Divisions, and Genl. Pack's Portugueze Brigade were selected. At eight o'clock the storming parties moved to the breaches while others escaladed the walls in different places. The first conflict was terrible. No description however, can do justice to the grandeur of the Scenery; the rapid fire of the Musketry, the infinite number of Hand Grenades, and the explosion of two Mines, presented a Coup d'Oeil beautifully awful. We had soon the satisfaction of hearing our brave Fellows give the cheer of Victory, a Victory however dearly purchased; I have not yet seen the amount of our loss, but it is said that the Siege and assault together cost us not less than seven hundred men, and a number of excellent Officers. Genl. MacKinnon was killed by the explosion of one of the mines; Genl. Crawfurd Comg. the Light Division and Col. Colburne of the 52d, who so gallantly stormed the redoubt on the first Evening, are both dangerously wounded; their deaths would indeed be a national loss. The Governor had no right to stand the assault; he had not the means after the breaches were practicable of defending himself against our superior numbers. By the laws of war, we should have been justified in putting the whole Garrison to death; they were almost all however suffered to escape with their lives; this was at best but a milk and water humanity, and in point of policy should be severely condemned: we may live to lament the effects of it.

The unfortunate inhabitants, as is ever the case on such occasions, were shamefully plundered by our Troops; in fact, no distinction was made by them between French and Spaniards; gallant as are our soldiers when opposed to an Enemy, I fear they yield to no people on earth in their thirst for plunder.

It is almost impossible sufficiently to appreciate the value of this achievement; its conception on the part of Lord W. at this season of the Year, was most admirable, and perhaps exceeds in brilliancy all his former exploits. In justice to every Department of the Army it must be stated that their exertions were unparallelled. The Siege lasted only eleven days, & the place was taken after five Days of open Trenches; whereas the French when they took it had been besieging it for six weeks, and did not get possession of it till after seventeen Days of open Trenches.

Marmont is said to be advancing upon us with fifty thousand Men, but it is probable that when he hears of the fall of the place he will retrace his steps. In the meantime we have resumed our Cantonments in Villa de Porco, where we are likely to remain till it is ascertained whether the French General will continue to advance or not.

26. Head Quarters were to have moved this Day to Frenada, but in consequence of the enemy manifesting a disposition to advance they remain for the present at Gallegos.

I was yesterday at Ciudad Rodrigo, and was much astonished to observe the wonderful progress that has been already made in repairing the Breaches; the place is now as inaccessible to an assault as it was the first Day we appeared before it. While there I witnessed the funeral of Genl. Crawford, who died of his wound the preceding Day; it was a very solemn and impressive ceremony, almost every Officer of Rank in the Army being present; he was buried close to the small Breach, on the Spot where he received his wound; he is considered a real loss to the Service, tho' from the peculiarity of his disposition it is said he had attached but few People to him.

30th. It would appear that the Enemy are gone back, but Head Quarters still remain at Gallegos. The disposition for a general change of Cantonments is made out, and will, it is supposed, be carried into effect in a day or two. The rainy Season has effectually set in, which will prevent the Enemy from commencing active Operations in this quarter for some time.

The Battering Trains employed by the French in the reduction of Ciudad Rodrigo have been found there with an infinite quantity of Stores of every description. It seems to have been the chief depôt of the Enemy's Northern Army.

Feb. 5. We are detained in our present Cantonments by the very heavy rains that have prevailed the last three days ; in Consequence the small Rivers in our rear called the Duas Casas & Turon are absolutely impassable ; should the bad weather continue, it is difficult to conceive how the Army will receive their supplies.

Head Quarters are returned to Frenada, & the repairs at Ciudad Rodrigo go on with activity ; it is the intention of Lord Wellington to make it much stronger than it ever was ; for this purpose, the Fort of San Francisco taken on the Evening of the 8th is to be considerably enlarged and a new Fort is to be erected on an eminence in front of the old one on a spot where it was intended our breaching Battery should have been, had we not succeeded in breaching from our first parallel.

9th. We have at length received our Route, and march at daylight to-morrow morning ; our destination is Punhete on the Tagus, where we shall be able to get our Clothing & every article of equipment of which we stand very much in need. The other part of the Brigade remains in this Neighbourhood for the present.

20th. We marched according to orders on the 10th Inst. and reached Aldea de Ponte, five Leagues, the same day, where we joined the Brigade in the 1st Division under the Command of Genl. Stopford, with whom it was intended we should proceed. At Night however a counter Order was received and we were directed to return the following day to Villa Formosa & there wait for Orders : this arrangement was in consequence of our Clothing having left Abrantes, & being considerably advanced on its Route towards us. On the 12th we marched to Villa de Ciervo, where we still remain : it is a very good Cantonment, and was Head Quarters of the Division at the time we lay at Gallegos. We do not expect however to be long here. It is notorious that the utmost exertions are making to commence again the Siege of Badajos, and as it is a Fortress of such vast importance the Enemy will doubtless make every effort to relieve it, and it will of course be necessary for Lord Wellington to have his whole Force in that Quarter. Unhappily we still continue very Sickly, & it is to be feared that, whatever may be our numerical strength, our physical force will be found most lamentably short of it. Head Quarters still remain at Frenada, tho' it is said they will remove in a very few Days to Castello Branco.

[MARCH]   March 3d.   We quitted Villa de Ciervo on the 27th Ulto. having received a route to proceed to Castello Branco : we reached Alamanda that day & halted there.   On the 28th we halted at Villa Mayor : 29th at Villa Boa ; & on the 1st Inst. we crossed the Coa at Sabugal & halted at a village called St. Estevão : our march yesterday was a very long and painful one, being five Leagues : we remained for the night at Pedrogão, & this day came to St. Miguel, only two Leagues & good road.   On our arrival at Castello Branco, we shall receive a fresh route : we know we are to go to Portalegre, & it is expected we shall remain there a short time.   There is no doubt that Lord W. purposes besieging Badajos, tho' it is probable there may be a previous general engagement, as the Deserters who have come in within these few days concur in stating that Marmont is marching his whole force Southward.

12th.   On the 4th we halted at a small village called Escalhas de Cima, and the following day reached Castel Branco, at which place we halted on the 6th.   On the 7th we remained at a most wretched place called Requisa, which scarcely afforded Covering for one fourth of the Men.   On the 8th we had a most fatiguing march to Nisa a distance of five

Leagues & a half over the worst roads in Portugal, added to which, we had the dragging of the Nine Pounders up two most tremendous Hills ; the Men came in so exhausted in the Evening, that we have had much accession to our Sick List since in consequence. On the 9th we halted at Alpalhão, our third visit to this place : on the 10th we reached Portalegre, where we still remain, tho' it is probable we shall march in the direction of Badajos in a day or two. Head Quarters left this place yesterday Morning for Elvas, where there is to be this day a grand installation, Genls. Hill & Graham being to be made Knights of the Bath. Everything is said to be ready for the Siege, & the weather continues remarkably fine.

The probability of a general Action increases. The advanced Guard of the enemy is said to have reached Merida ; a few days therefore will in all probability develop great events.

22d. On the 14th we received a sudden Order to quit Portalegre & proceed in the direction of Elvas ; we reached Monforte, a clean and pretty Town that day, and on the following day arrived at Elvas. There we found the dispositions of the Army were as follows ; the 1st, 2nd, 6th, & 7th Divisions, with almost the whole of the Cavalry and Horse Artillery, formed the covering Army, and were to proceed upon Villa Franca near Zafra (at which place the enemy had a Corps), by two separate Routes under the orders of Sir Thos. Graham & Sir Rowland Hill; the Light 3d & 4th Divisions formed the besieging Army. The whole moved on the following morning (16th). On the same day Badajos was invested, & ground was broke on the Evening of the 17th. A vast deal of work has been since done, but no Guns have as yet been placed in the Batteries, neither is it known when our Fire will open. On the 18th the enemy made a Sortie, but were almost immediately driven in without our works sustaining the smallest injury ; the fire was very sharp & our loss amounted to about twenty killed & a hundred wounded ;

amongst the latter was Col. Fletcher, the Chief Engineer ; fortunately however it has not altogether deprived the Army of his valuable Services. The loss of the Enemy is said to have been double.

On the very day that we invested the place the wind shifted to the S.W. It has rained ever since almost without intermission. Lord W. and the whole of Headquarters are encamped.

We know not whether the enemy can concentrate in sufficient force to compel us to raise the siege : the Corps they had at Zafra retired on the approach of Genls. Graham & Hill.

It is stated that the Engineers calculate that it will require three weeks from this time to reduce the place, but it is generally supposed that their real opinion is it will be effected in a fortnight.

25th. The wind changed yesterday Evening to the Northward, and the weather now promises to be fine. For seven days it was dreadful, the rains being so excessively heavy, that it became at length extremely disheartening.

Our Batteries opened this day at ten o'Clock : it is said that Fort Piccolini, a work of considerable importance, will be stormed to-night ; it is highly essential to the success of our enterprise that it should be in our possession.

26th. At eight o'Clock last Night the Fort was stormed in a Stile of unexampled Gallantry by the Covering Parties of the 3d Division. Independent of its strength, they had a variety of obstacles to overcome, & the resistance made by the enemy was very great. They succeeded however in surmounting all the difficulties. The French, being reinforced from the Town, attempted to retake the place, but were repulsed with great slaughter. The Fire from the Enemy's Batteries during the business exceeded anything I ever witnessed. Our loss in this important Conquest was about an hundred & fifty ;

that of the Enemy was certainly more than double. Their loss was principally in killed ; several Officers & about eighty Men were made Prisoners.

The weather continues fine, & everything appears to augur a successful issue to the Siege.

30th. The first breaching battery opened this Morning, and the remainder will commence their fire to-morrow ; it is confidently expected that the place will fall by the 4th, tho' it is generally apprehended that it must be taken by Storm ; should this be the case it is scarcely to be conceived the Enemy will come off so well as they did at Ciudad Rodrigo.

It is known that a large French force is advancing to the relief of the Garrison, but it is supposed that they cannot possibly arrive here before the 10th.

Apl. 2. The Breach is in a considerable state of forwardness, and appears to be fifty or sixty yards wide ; the wall was found exceedingly tough, and it is only this Afternoon that they have well got to the Earth ; eighteen Guns from two Batteries are constantly playing upon it, & it is hoped that on the day after to-morrow it will be perfectly practicable. Besides the great Breach a second is making from an Eight Gun Battery, the effect of which is I believe still more advanced than the other. The Fire from the Enemy is very great ; they have brought between thirty & forty guns to bear upon our works ; the Batteries of course are much injured by them, but the Casualties amongst the Men are very few.

A very desperate resistance is apprehended at the Storming. It is impossible to anticipate the carnage that must ensue without feelings of the utmost horror ; no idea is entertained of a Capitulation, indeed it is one of the fundamental rules of the Code Napoleon, that any Governor giving up a Fortress without standing the assault shall be shot.

We have heard nothing further respecting the advance of Soult. Genls. Graham & Hill have with them thirty thousand men, which probably may be sufficient to keep him in check. It is reported that Marmont is making preparations for the Siege of Rodrigo, but such a rumour appears too absurd to be entitled to any credit.

5th. Both Breaches were considered practicable last Night, and it was generally apprehended that the Storm would take place. There is no doubt that the assault will be made either this Evening or before daylight to-morrow Morning. Everything is ready. The Town has not been summoned, and it is supposed will not; it is said that Lord Wellington is unwilling to subject himself to an insolent reply.

The assault will be made by the three Divisions that have been employed during the Siege; viz. the Light, 3rd, & 4th; the Light Divn. are to storm the small breach, the 4th the large One and the 3rd are to Escalade the Castle walls.

All idea or probability of an early visit from Soult or Marmont appears at an end; the former it is said left Seville with his Army in this direction, but again retrograded after two days March. Marmont is reported to have actually invested Rodrigo; he is without heavy Artillery to commence a regular Siege, but is supposed to found his hopes of again getting possession of the place from its not being provisioned sufficiently; should this actually be the case, it would seem absolutely necessary that we should again go to the North for the purpose of raising the Blockade.

10th. The period that has elapsed since the last date has been a truly eventful one, and will certainly long hold a place in the recollection of those who have witnessed it and yet survive. The assault did not take place on the night of the 5th, as was fully expected. Orders for the Attack were actually issued when about five in the Evening they were countermanded. A third Breach was determined upon, which was effected in the course of the following Day; the Attack was then ordered to take place at ten o'clock the same Night

(6th). One Breach was given to the Light Division, two to the 4th. The 3rd were ordered to scale the Walls of the Castle, and a Brigade of the 5th to escalade the walls of the Town near the Olivenza Gate. At the appointed hour the Troops moved to their respective Posts, when a scene of horror at once dreadful and sublime presented itself. There was no Moon but the stars afforded just sufficient light to enable the Men to find their respective destinations. On their being discovered by the Enemy, a Fire so tremendous opened on them, that the oldest Military Men present declare that they never witnessed anything that could be at all compared to it. The explosions from the several Mines the Enemy had prepared were indescribably awful, but certainly furnished a Coup d'Oeil such as I never expect or indeed wish again to witness. The access to the Breach was most difficult from the Countercarp not having been blown in ; it was necessary to descend into the Ditch by means of Ladders ; on reaching it, it was found full of water, and in some places it was so deep that the Men were drowned in it ; on gaining the summit of the Breach, obstacles the most insurmountable presented themselves ; Chevaux de frise made of swords were placed the whole length in the rear of the Breach, and further in the Rear Trenches upon Trenches were cut ; repeated attempts were made to get in but our People were as constantly repelled, with the most horrible loss. The Escalades were at length successful, which so much attracted the Enemy's attention from the Breaches, that the men were enabled to get in, and the Garrison was surrounded. In the meantime the Governor (Philippon) had fled to St. Christoval, but finding it impossible to make any effectual resistance he surrendered at discretion. The usual humanity of the English, was eminently displayed on this occasion, not a French Soldier was put to the sword, tho' according to the laws of war we should have been justified in putting every Soul to Death. It was about one o'Clock on the Morning of the 7th when our People got possession of the place. For the space of three hours, they had been exposed to the destructive fire I have before stated ; our loss was in consequence most melancholy, not less I believe than three thousand eight hundred killed & wounded besides at least two hundred and fifty Officers ; in my Regiment, twenty four Officers marched off from the Camp Ground, of which number only six escaped. Notwithstanding the extent of our loss, the taking of Badajos is considered as one of the most important events of the Peninsula ; it is of infinite consequence to the Spaniards, and it insures the safety of Portugal.

15th. On the 12th we marched from our encampment, and passing by Badajos halted at Campo Mayor. The following Day we bivouacked in the Neighbourhood of Arronches, and yesterday reached Portalegre. This morning we came to a most comfortable quarter called Castel de Vida, about two Leagues distant from Portalegre. We have no Orders as yet to continue our March to-morrow, but it is probable they will arrive in the course of the Evening, and that Nisa will be our next halting place ; the following day we expect to cross the Tagus. Every One is horrified at the idea of again going to the North, but it is rendered necessary by the Enemy taking advantage of our absence at the Siege of Badajos, & making incursions into Portugal in considerable force ; they entered Castel Branco, and, it is said, came as far as Villa Velha. It is to be feared we shall be kept continually in hot water between the two Fortresses of Badajos & Rodrigo : so much marching is disheartening in the extreme. The Army is far from healthy or rather that part of it employed in the late Siege ; the dreadful weather, aided by the horrid intemperance that took place after the assault, is making a melancholy ravage amongst the men ; till drunkenness becomes a punishable crime a British Army in the Peninsula never can be properly effective.

Since quitting Badajos we have received Accts. of an Affair between a Brigade of our Cavalry, and some Cavalry of the Enemy in which the latter were completely routed with the loss of seven or eight hundred in killed, wounded, and prisoners; our loss is not yet stated, but it is said to be comparatively very trifling.

18th. We remained the 16th at Castel de Vida, & yesterday marched to a most misèrable Village called Povoa das Meadas, where we still are. Tomorrow we cross the Tagus at Villa Velha, and proceed to Sarnadas, a wretched place about two Leagues on this side of Castel Branco. Head Quarters reached the latter place yesterday. We are entirely ignorant as to what is going on Northward, but from the slowing of our Movement it would not appear that Lord W. is under much apprehension respecting Almeida or Ciudad Rodrigo.

21st. We quitted Povoa on the 19th, & crossing the Tagus halted at Villa Velha. Yesterday we reached Castel Branco, and this day marched to Escalhas de Cima. It is understood that Marmont has about twenty five thousand Infantry, & two thousand Cavalry, a force altogether inadequate to make a stand against the number Lord W. can bring against him; Ciudad Rodrigo & Almeida are still in a state of Blockade, but the Governor of the former is said to have written to Lord W. stating his ability to hold out till the 1st of the month; it is supposed that as soon as a sufficient Convoy of Stores & Provisions shall be thrown into the place, we shall again go Southward.

The Enemy in their late incursion to this part of the country found the same determined hostility that they before experienced; not an individual remained in their Houses; everything that could possibly be serviceable to the French, that they could not carry away, they destroyed. Surely such a People never can be subdued; such unexampled patriotism must present a barrier more insurmountable than a wall of Adamant, to the iniquitous designs of their unprincipled Invaders.

25—On the 22d we halted at a small village called Aldea de Santa Margaritta, and on the 23d proceeded to Val de Lobo or the Valley of Wolves, a Village so called from the number of those Animals found in its Neighbourhood; yesterday we came to another wretched place called Quinta de Saint Bartholomew, and to our astonishment remain here to-day, nor have we any Orders to proceed further to-morrow. Head Quarters were yesterday at Alfayates, but we know nothing of them to-day; we are also entirely ignorant as to the movements of the Enemy: it is said, that Don Carlos has succeeded in destroying the Bridges over the Agueda, and that they cannot in consequence effect their retreat; this intelligence is to be doubted, as the Coa which is close to us here is perfectly fordable.

The Enemy have been in all the Villages thro' which we have lately passed, and it is impossible to describe the unprofitable mischief & devastation they have everywhere committed; the misery of the Inhabitants beggars description, indeed I cannot conceive how they will be able to support life.

[MAY]   May 2d—On the 26th we quitted Quinta San Bartholemew, which is close to Sabugal, & instead of crossing the Coa, as we expected, received a route to proceed in the direction of the Douro. The Enemy have entirely abandoned the Neighbourhood of Ciudad Rodrigo. On the 26th we halted at Parades, 27th, Lamegal, 28th, Cerejo; 29th Marialva; 30th Rehnadas, and yesterday arrived at our destination San Joaõ de Pesqueira, which is a small town about a league from the Douro. Here it is probable we shall remain for some time to recruit. The 3d & 5th Divisions are also in this Neighbourhood. Genl. Graham with the 1st 6th & 7th Divisions has marched again Southward, and Lord Wellington with the Light Division & 2 Regiments of Cavalry remained when we last heard in the Vicinity of Rodrigo.

We are much disappointed in this place, having heard it was an excellent Cantonment, and furnishing everything in abundance ; whereas it barely affords accommodation for two weak Regiments, and there is scarcely any single thing to be procured with the exception of wine.

12th. We remain still at San Joaõ de Pesqueira, nor is it probable that there will be any Movement in the Army till Rodrigo & Almeida are well provisioned. Head Quarters are yet at Guinaldo. Lord W. wrote to Genl. Pakenham who is ill in Lisbon, that the Spaniards had deceived him in not provisioning the former place according to promise, by which means he had been compelled to remove his Army Northward, and had in consequence lost the finest sport that ever any Troops had in view. As war has undoubtedly ere this taken place between France & Russia, it is probable that there will be a very active Campaign in this Country, & the South certainly would appear as the most likely part for the Scene of Action : it is generally expected therefore that we shall again move in that direction in the course of a very short time.

26th. Since my last date I have visited Oporto, attracted by the double motive of Curiosity, and the necessity of fitting myself out afresh with almost everything. I left this place (San Joaõ de Pesqueria) on the 16th, & returned yesterday, highly gratified by my Expedition. The distance from hence is about eighty miles. I was accompanied by a Friend ; we went by Water, but owing to unfavorable Winds we did not reach Oporto till the afternoon of the 18th. Our Horses & Servants went by Land ; the Navigation of the Douro is at all times somewhat perilous, and in the Winter is absolutely impracticable from the Rapidity of the current, & the number of concealed Rocks. The Scenery on some parts of the River is fine beyond all description ; never before did I so much regret not being a Draughtsman. Oporto itself is a very large & populous Town, being the second in Portugal : it is most beautifully situated, and in point of comfort is superior to any I ever saw out of England ; indeed it resembles an English Town more than I could have possibly expected. It is infinitely cleaner than Lisbon, and superior to it in every respect ; like Lisbon however it abounds in Churches & Convents, and the number of Monks parading the Streets is absolutely disgusting. The Theatre is a very elegant one, but the Performers are wretched. I had the gratification of seeing that part of the Douro, which was the scene of Lord W.'s brilliant exploit in April 1809, when Soult fled with such precipitation before him. The Inhabitants are excessively loyal, & his Lordship is little less than a Divinity in their estimation.

We quitted Oporto on the afternoon of the 22d, and rode to Penafiel, a large Town distant six Leagues ; here we found a good hotel, kept by a Black. On the 23d we rode to Amaranthe, four leagues ; from this place the Portuguese General Silveira takes his Title of Count. It is impossible that any Situation can be more truly beautiful, but the French having met with an unusual resistance from the Portugueze Militia, headed by Sylveira about three years since, on gaining possession of the Town they entirely destroyed it, with the exception of a large Convent of the Dominican Order. At this Convent we were entertained by the Monks, & though there was the appearance of Hospitality, it was that niggardly sort of hospitality, that leaves no impression of gratitude on the Mind. On the 24th we rode seven Leagues to a Village about six Leagues from hence, where we were comfortably entertained in the house of a Fidalgo. The Fidalgos in Portugal are a set of superior Gentry, and have in general more pride than the Nobility ; the word Fidalgo, is derived from Filho de Algo, which in English may be literally translated Son of Somebody. Yesterday we rejoined our Regiment and find there is a general expectation of an early move, though various opinions as to its direction ; some thinking we

[1812]
[MAY] shall march immediately Southward, while others conceive we shall in the first instance make a dash at Salamanca, & then proceed South by the way of Placentia.

[JUNE]   June 3d. We still remain at Pesqueira; English Papers to the 11th Ulto. have been received, which do not furnish anything very interesting, but a private letter from London of the 12th mentions the assassination of Mr. Percival in the Lobby of the House of Commons the preceding Evening. There is something so truly dreadful in this proceeding, that the reflection on it I find attended with an horror I never before experienced. Independent of the great loss I conceive the Nation to have sustained by their deprivation of Mr. P.'s talents & integrity, I fear this diabolical act is the precursor of much woe & bloodshed to England : the Country appears ripe for mischief, & I have a melancholy presage that she is about to bleed at every pore. It is impossible not to consider this most foul murder as a visitation from Heaven on a guilty land ; England, blessed beyond other Nations by her insular situation, and consequently a stranger to the horrors of war, is at length I fear about to become a prey to all the accumulated woes of internal discord. The long-suffering of the Almighty, so visibly displayed in her exemption from those miseries, that for so many years have afflicted Continental Europe, has never been remembered by her with a gratitude proportionate to mercies so distinguished ; on the contrary these blessings of Heaven have been received with the same unthankfulness as they were by the Israelites of old, and to us may justly be applied the passage of the Prophet, " Shall I not visit for these things, saith the Lord, and shall not my soul be avenged on such a Nation as this ? " That England, is about to suffer for her manifold iniquities, I can have no doubt, but I indulge the hope that the Mercy of Heaven may be yet extended to her, from the consolatory reflection that she still retains within her Bosom her " Seven thousand, who have not yet bowed the Knee to Baal."

Great exertions are making to complete a Depôt forming on the Douro not far from Almeida ; it is generally supposed we shall then march, and that the operations of the Army will be carried on with a degree of activity unparallelled in the Annals of Military History ; tho' it is to be feared the lamented death of Mr. Percival, by introducing a new set of Men into the Cabinet, (& consequently new Measures) may tend to paralyze the exertions of Lord Wellington. For my own part I indulge the hope that the new Administration will be formed by Lord Wellesly, in which case the war in this Country may be expected to be carried on with ever increased vigour.

Genl. Hill it seems has been again successful, taking the Bridge at Almaraz by a Coup de Main, with loss to the Enemy of upwards of five hundred men and a very large depôt of Stores etc. etc. Our loss on this occasion is said to be about one hundred in killed & wounded.

6th. On the Evening of the 3rd a Route was received, directing us to quit San Joāo de Pesqueira on the 5th Inst. & march to a large wood near Espeja, & about three Leagues from Ciudad Rodrigo. We reached Rehnadas yesterday, & were to have proceeded on our March this day, for which purpose we fell in at 4 o'Clock this morning : just as we were about to set off, an Order was received to remain at Rehnadas to-day, & to go on according to route to-morrow. This delay is said [to] be occasioned by the Road we are to go not being clear of another Division of the Army.

We are ignorant of the object of our march to Espeja, but we hear that the whole Army is to rendezvous there, with the exception of the 2d Division ; if this be the case there can be no doubt that we are going against Salamanca ; the Enemy are said to have collected immense Magazines in that place.

On the 7th we quitted Rehnadas and halted at a small Village called Cotinos. On the 8th we reached Pinhel, formerly a very neat Town but at present bearing the most deplorable

marks of French devastation; it is a Bishop's See, but his
Excellency's House is entirely devasted.   On the 9th we
marched to Aldea de Bispa; & the morning of the 10th
proceeded according to route in the direction of Espeja.   On
reaching Alamada, we received an order to bivouack in the
wood near that place; it was generally understood the Division
would be viewed by Lord W. on this day, but yesterday
evening we were directed to proceed by Gallegos, & cross the
river Agueda at the Bridge of Marialva.   We are encamped
about a league from Ciudad Rodrigo & it appears to be
generally understood we shall march immediately upon
Salamanca without any delay whatever.

14th.   On the 12th we halted, & yesterday crossed the
Agueda at Ciudad Rodrigo & proceeded three Leagues beyond
that place on the Salamanca road; we bivouacked in a wood
near a small Village called Santispiritus.   This day we have
had a march of four Leagues and are in bivouack in a beautiful wood near San Muñoz; we are at present nine Leagues
from Salamanca.   It is confidently reported the Enemy have
quitted the place, which may make a difference in our movements; should they be Northward it would appear hazardous
to follow them, as Lisbon would then be open to the incursions
of Soult & Suchet.

The weather is so intensely hot, that it is scarcely
supportable.

15.   We marched to-day three leagues thro' a beautiful
Country and are encamped in the Neighbourhood of a Village
called Cojos de Robliza.   It does not appear that the enemy
have as yet quitted Salamanca, tho' from several movements
there is reason to believe they do not purpose making a stand
there.

Our Army moves in three Columns.   The centre
comprised of the 4th, 5th, & Light Divisions, with the 1st
Hussars, 12th & 16th Dragoons, and heavy German Brigade,

is more immediately under the command of Lord Wellington in Person ; the right, consisting of the 1st, 6th, & 7th Divisions, with the 14th Dragoons, is commanded by Sir Thos. Graham ; & the left, of the 3rd Division, Genl Pack's & Bradford's Portugueze Brigades, with the 11th Light Dragoons & Genl. Le Marchant's Heavy Brigade, are under the command of Genl. Picton. Lord W. is gone to reconnoitre as near as possible ; on his return it is probable the orders that will be then issued will give us some insight into his intentions.

16. We are in bivouack about a League & a half from Salamanca. There has been some skirmishing to-day in which we lost three Officers, & a few men wounded. Marmont is supposed to be still there, with about a thousand Cavalry and five thousand Infantry, but it is probable they will go off to-night, leaving a Garrison in two very strongly fortified Convents, which it is thought may give us some trouble. By a variety of intercepted Letters it appears that they have an intrenched camp, a short distance on this side of Valladolid, where they will be able to concentrate near forty thousand men, & where they purpose making a stand. Our force is about the same, added to which we are to be joined by twenty thousand Spaniards under Castaños. There is said to be little danger from Soult & Suchet, Lord W. having combined a plan of operations in the South, that will keep them fully employed.

26th. The Enemy went off on the night of the 16th, leaving seven or eight hundred men in the Convent of [San Vincente] which is fortified by several strong works. On the Morning of the 17th the whole Army moved to their front ; Genl. Graham's & Picton's Columns crossed the Tormes by two Fords one above & the other below the River [? Town] ; the 6th Division entered the Town, & the 4th & 5th Divisions bivouacked in a wood near the Ford where Genl. Picton's Column crossed. As the Convent the enemy possessed commanded the Bridge, without which Lord W. could not move forward his Army with safety, preparations were immediately made for commencing the Siege of it. Ground was broke that Night as near as possible ; on the 19th our Batteries opened, but from a scarcity of Ammunition no great impression was made on the Works ; the Fire from the enemy was excessively galling and our loss considerable, particularly in Artillery. On the morning of the 20th we received a sudden Order to cross the River & advance, the Enemy having appeared in force about three Leagues distant. Lord W. took up an extremely advantageous position within a League of the Town, & in the Afternoon the two Armies were in sight of each other ; some skirmishing took place. A portion of the 6th Division remained in the Town, but the Siege was for a time converted into a Blockade. On the 21st there was a general expectation that we should be attacked, but the day passed with a little skirmishing only ; in the Afternoon the Enemy were observed to receive considerable reinforcements. On the 22d at Day Break they were found to have possession of a Hill which threatened our right ; they were in consequence attacked and driven from it by the 7th Division, with the loss of about 70 Men on our side : Marshal Marmont was observed extremely busy the whole day in reconnoitring. At Daylight on the 23d they were not to be seen, and it appeared they went off about 11 o'Clock the preceding Night. They did not retrograde much, but brought up on some Hills about a League distant. The remainder of the 6th Division were again ordered into town, and in the Afternoon our Batteries recommenced firing. In the Evening the Enemy were observed crossing Troops over the River ; in consequence of which Genl. Graham crossed likewise. At night the Enemy's works in Town were twice attempted to be stormed, but both attacks failed, as is said thro' the shortness of the ladders ; on this occasion Genl. Bowes was killed, and our total loss was several Officers, and about 130 men. On the 24th the whole Army moved to its right, the Enemy having made a parallel movement to their left : they had about 10,000 men across the river, to which Force Lord W. opposed some Cavalry & the 1st Division; a slight skirmishing only took place; in the afternoon the Enemy again retired, and are brought up a League from us, where they still remain. There is no doubt they are anxious to relieve the Garrison in Town and are manoeuvring for that purpose. Their force is supposed to be nearly equal to ours, but on these terms they do not appear willing to attack. It is generally understood they will be joined to-morrow by Bonnet from the Asturias, which will probably give them a numerical superiority over us of nearly eight or ten thousand men. A general confidence however prevails that the result will be glorious to the allied Arms, should there be a general conflict. Of the Spanish Northern Army under Castaños we have a thousand contradictory reports, it is natural to suppose however, they are somehow or other acting in concert with us.—Accounts from the South state that on the 20th & 21st Genl. Hill & Soult were drawn up opposite to each other at Albuhera without coming to action; it is reported that General Hill has since retired upon Portalegre, but this requires confirmation.

Salamanca is a very delightful Town, but has suffered considerably from French protection. The Colleges are all destroyed. The Cathedral is an exquisite structure; it has nothing gaudy in its interior but the Architecture is superbly magnificent; it is impossible sufficiently to admire it and as impossible to convey by the Pen any adequate idea of its beauty; the Enemy have thrown a few shells into it, but it is hitherto little injured.—That part of the Inhabitants in the French Interest quitted the Town with the Enemy; they are said to comprise about one hundred & twenty five families. Those who remain appear extremely loyal, and hailed the entrance of British Troops into their city with the loudest acclamations. There is at present however a great despondency among them from the circumstance of the enemy hovering in the Neighbourhood, and the consequent possibility that they may again take

possession of the Town. The present period is certainly an
eventful one; on the issue of the next few days in all probability depends the question, whether Spain shall or shall not
be free.

30th. The firing continued against the Fort all day of
the 26th with considerable effect; in the evening red hot Shot
were thrown which succeeded in setting Fire to the Convent
which however was got under; at Night a storming party fell
in, and were on the point of moving off, when they were
countermanded. On the Morning of the 27th the Convent
was again set on fire; it burned with considerable violence and
evidently could not be subdued; the breach in the works was
also considered practicable. Under these circumstances,
Lord W. summoned the Enemy, who refused to surrender;
the storming party which was previously ready immediately
advanced, when the Enemy held out a white Flag, & the several
Forts were taken possession of without resistance; the number
of Prisoners made was between six & seven hundred. The
Town was instantly in a tumult of joy, & were it not for the
protection afforded by the British, the French would certainly
have fallen Victims to the Ferocity of the Lower Orders of the
Inhabitants. The 28th was completely a Gala Day, and the
satisfaction of the People was in no small degree enhanced by
the circumstance of the Enemy having gone off the preceding
night. The Cathedral was magnificently decorated, & Te Deum
performed at which Lord W. attended in state; at night the
Town was illuminated. The Square in Salamanca is one of
the handsomest in Europe, and the lights on this occasion
being extremely numerous, rendered it uncommonly beautiful.

Yesterday Morning the whole Army marched, and this day
continued their route; we are at present six Leagues from
Salamanca, but are altogether ignorant what is our destination.
Valladolid is generally supposed to be the place we are going
to, but it is not improbable the enemy will avail themselves of
the extremely strong position of Toro, which may give us some

trouble to force. The Country we pass through is highly fertile, but the Corn is everywhere lamentably destroyed. The Villages have been systematically plundered by the Enemy, the Churches destroyed, and vast numbers of Houses burnt to the ground; indeed the same scenes present themselves, that we witnessed in Portugal on the retreat of Massena. It would really appear from these horrible devastations that they have little hope or expectation of speedily returning to this part of the Country. Official accounts from the South state that Soult has retired, being unwilling to risk an action with the Force under General Hill.

[July]   July 3d. We continued our route towards Valladolid yesterday and the preceding day. We halted yesterday near a considerable Town called Medina del Campo, where we still remain. Of the cause of the halt we are entirely ignorant. There was some skirmishing yesterday, in which the Enemy lost about thirty men; ours was very trifling. We have heard some firing to-day on the left, but know not what was the cause or consequence of it. Medina is a large and very old town, standing on the high Road from Madrid to Corunna. Its population before the war was about twelve thousand, but it is at present greatly deserted. This being the first time a British Force has been there, the people are remarkably civil; they have had a French Garrison in the place from the very first day it was occupied by them.

The enemy have abandoned Toro, leaving a small Garrison there; it is probable however we shall not trouble ourselves about them. It lies off the Road to Valladolid, where their principal force is. Medina is distant from Madrid thirty Leagues, and from Valladolid eight.

7th. There has been no move since my last date. Our inactivity proceeds from an impossibility of crossing the Douro. The Enemy have destroyed the several bridges over it, with the exception of that at Tordesillas, which is so strongly fortified that it cannot be forced. There are different

Fords, but they are all too deep to admit of the passage of Artillery or Baggage. It is probable steps are taking for the construction of a Bridge, but, if so, it is not generally known. It is rumoured that it is not intended that the Army should move in the direction of Valladolid, but that on the junction of Castaños the Spaniards should remain to watch the Salamanca Road, while Lord W. makes a flank movement to his right, which appears to mean nothing more or less than moving directly upon the Capital.

Head quarters are at Rueda, a distance of two short Leagues from Tordesillas, and our advanced Posts are about three hundred yards from those of the Enemy.—The weather is most oppressively hot, and such is the nature of this part of the Country, that it is altogether impossible to procure wood or any other substance for the purpose of sheltering the troops from the excessive power of the Sun.

10. Head quarters remain at Rueda, & there have been no material changes in the Army. We moved last night at Midnight one League, for the purpose of occupying ground vacated by the 5th & 6th Divisions, who are gone I know not where ; it was adviseable that this move should not be overlooked by the Enemy. We lie about equal distance between the Towns of Rueda and Nava. In point of shelter we are not a bit better off than we were before.

There appears no probability of our soon seeing Valladolid. It is said that Lord Wellington has gained his end, in having dispossessed the Enemy of all the fine Corn Country throughout the province of Salamanca, and extending along the Tagus as far as Talavera de la Reyna. The concentration of all their force to oppose us will likewise afford a splendid opportunity to the Guerillas, of which no doubt they will not fail to avail themselves.

We hear from deserters that Bonnet has joined, and that Caffarelli with a considerable force is coming from Navarre ; on his junction it is supposed we shall be attacked.

Sir Thomas Graham has been compelled from ill health to quit the Army, and is gone home to the great regret of everybody: conjecture says that he will be succeeded by Sir Edw. Paget, a very deservedly popular Officer. The present second in command is Sir Stapleton Cotton, an officer who has some knowledge of Cavalry Movements, but who is entirely inexperienced in all the detail necessary to make a good Commander in Chief. It would indeed be dreadful, were anything now to happen to Lord W.; to say the least of it, the safety of the Army would be endangered.

16th. In consequence of the enemy making a movement to their right yesterday, & concentrating a large force opposite the Ford at Pollos, where the 3d Division are stationed, Lord Wellington moved his troops to their left in order to be able to support that Division in case of their being attacked; Head Quarters also were changed from Rueda to a place called Nava del Rey about two leagues further to the left. As it was not unlikely that the enemy would this morning attempt to force the Ford at Pollos, we were under Arms an hour before Daylight to be in readiness. Everything however remained very quiet, & about seven we took up our ground on some heights, near to those we quitted last night, the Light Division occupying those we left. We have now been a fortnight in this neighbourhood, and we are still unable to form an idea when we shall be able to advance. The very strong position of the Enemy renders them secure from our Attack, and notwithstanding the arrival of their reinforcements they appear as unwilling to attack us. In the meantime a singular mode of warfare is carried on; it is not uncommon to see five hundred of the Enemy, and as many of our men, bathing together in the Douro in the most perfect good humour possible, at the same time that the Cavalry of the two rival Armies come down on their respective sides of the River to water, it being perfectly understood that neither party shall ever approach the River armed. Any infringement of this agreement is noticed by firing on any armed Cavalry or Infantry of either side.

21st   On the Evening of the 16th we received a sudden order to march to Villa Verde, a village about a Mile in rear of Medina del Campo; this movement was occasioned by the Enemy having in the Afternoon crossed the Douro on our left.   On reaching Villa Verde we were directed to proceed near three leagues further to a place called Castrejon, on the Salamanca Road, which we did not reach till after daylight of the 17th.   We remained there the whole of that day, and the enemy advanced as far as Nava del Rey, about five miles from us.   Early on the 18th skirmishing commenced, & about six o'clock the French appeared in great force.   As our Army was not concentrated we fell back upon the Divisions in our rear, and as was understood into the neighbourhood of a position Lord Wellington meant to meet them in.   During the day there were several severe skirmishes, and amongst others some most furious charges of Cavalry; the enemy had two opportunities of cannonading, which they availed themselves of most vigorously, but happily our loss was but little.   I was myself very nearly being one of the Victims, a Cannon Shot passing within a few inches of my head. The enemy pressed us in a manner, and with a spirit, we were never before accustomed to.   At length, a favorable opportunity occurring, Lord W. directed the 4th Division to attack their advanced guard; as the Attack was made by the Division left in front, it fell to the 27th & 40th Regts composing the left Brigade to bear the brunt of the affair.   These two regiments, on approaching the Enemy, advanced to the charge in the most undaunted manner, notwithstanding the force opposed to them was near three times their number; the French presented a firm front, till our People arrived within about twenty paces of them, when they fired a volley, and flew in the utmost confusion. Unfortunately, the assailants were so much exhausted from a long previous march, and the great heat of the weather (which was so excessive that several men and officers actually died on the march), that they were unable to follow them up as could have been wished. The business was soon over with a loss to the Division of 5 Officers killed and wounded, and about two hundred men, of which one Officer and seventy [Men] belonged to my Regiment: the loss of the Enemy was estimated at upwards of six hundred Men. After this Affair the Enemy did not attempt to advance a step, but took up a position, while we did the same.—We remained in position on the 19th till the Evening, when the French were observed moving in force to their left, the British Army in consequence moved to their right, and head quarters were established for the night at Villase.—At dawn of day on the morning of the 20th the whole British Army was formed in order of Battle on an immense plain, which was as fair a Challenge to the Enemy as could possibly be given; they however declined it and continued to move to their left; we were again necessarily put in motion, and moved parallel with them. We halted about Noon near a Village, three Leagues from Salamanca, the Enemy being in position between us and the Tormes—At daylight this Morning, we marched in the direction of Salamanca, and are now bivouacked on the Tormes about a mile from that City. Genl. Picton with a column is on our old position, to prevent the Enemy getting possession of it; Genl. Clinton with the 6th Division is across the River, observing the Motions of a part of the French Army that went over yesterday Evening, and the remainder of our force are along the banks of the River, to be ready to cross it or move to the position, according as the motions of the Enemy shall render one or the other necessary—Thus without fighting a battle have they compelled us to retrograde all the way from the Douro to this place, and it is even now very doubtful whether we shall be able to maintain ourselves at Salamanca, as in the event of their continuing to move to their left, we must of necessity move parallel with them, and uncover it. I have not been into the Town, but I hear the utmost consternation prevails there at the idea of again having the French with them. Events may yet turn out well, but at present I fear we have gained but little popularity by our irruption into the North of Spain.

26th. The events since my last date have been of an importance altogether unprecedented since the commencement of hostilities in this Country. On the Evening of the 21st it having been ascertained that nearly the whole of the French army had passed the Tormes, the British army crossed it likewise, and took up a position about a League from Salamanca having our left upon the River. At daybreak on the 22d we discovered the enemy posted on the heights opposite us. They very soon sent out a large party of Dragoons, & Sharpshooters, and a very smart skirmish commenced, which lasted for two or three hours ; this was not with any intention of subsequently attacking us, but merely to cover a movement of their Army to their left. In the course of the forenoon they had occupied some most advantageous heights, near a league further to their left ; & while they were able from their immense Artillery & apparently impregnable position to cannonade us with effect, it reduced Lord W. to the necessity of either uncovering Salamanca, or allowing them to get on the Ciudad Rodrigo Road in which latter case our Baggage would have been taken, and our supplies intercepted. His Lordship therefore (notwithstanding their advantageous position) resolved to attack them. The Attack commenced about four o'Clock in the afternoon, and continued till eight at night, when the Enemy were dislodged from their heights, and pursued in the utmost confusion. They recrossed the river the same night at Alba de Tormes, & the Head Quarters of the British Army were established at that place. On the 23d the pursuit continued, when a great number of Prisoners were made ; the Brigade of Heavy Germans made a charge upon two solid Columns and took fifteen hundred Prisoners. On the 24th the Army continued to move forward. Yesterday we were compelled to halt in order to enable the Stores & Provisions of the Army to reach us. This day we marched four Leagues, and are at present about ten from Salamanca; we are ignorant where Head Quarters are this Evening.

The battle of the 22d was crowned by the completest Victory on record. The French lost several General officers, five Eagles, twenty pieces of Artillery, a great quantity of Baggage, & about fifteen thousand Men ; the loss on our part is between three & four thousand. Genl. Le Marchant is killed & Genls. Beresford, Leith, Cole & Alten wounded ; the Divisions employed on this memorable day were the 3d, 4th, 5th, & 6th, the Light, 1st & 7th Divisions being in reserve. The whole business was performed by the Bayonet, & the most sceptical must now be surely convinced how superior in the use of it is the British Soldier to every other in the world. Among the French General officers wounded was Marshal Marmont, the Commander in Chief ; he had an arm amputated at Alba de Tormes, and received besides another wound ; the operation was of necessity hastily performed, and he left that place in the greatest agitation of mind. It is reported he is since dead, & the event is extremely probable ; perhaps it were better for him that such were the case, as his reputation as a great General by this late business has received a mortal stab. Lord W. on the contrary, has by this achievement placed himself almost beyond the reach of rivalry. Splendid as are his military talents, he must consider himself in great measure indebted to his success from his good fortune in commanding the bravest Troops in the world ; men who when well led on will hesitate at nothing. It is to be hoped that some pen equal to the task will describe the heroic Acts of the 22d, & thus do justice to that valour which may almost be considered as romantic.

28th. Yesterday we marched two Leagues & a half, & bivouacked near a village called Castillejos on the River Zapadiel. This day we have come the same distance, & are encamped on the same River, near the village of San Vicente del Palacio ; Head Quarters are at a Town called Olmedo, about two Leagues in front of us, and on the high road from Madrid to Valladolid. It is confidently rumoured that the junction of the Enemy with their reinforcements from Madrid has been prevented and that their advanced Guard has been fallen in with and defeated by our Cavalry; King Joseph is said to be with them. The Road we have marched on this time has been very far to the left of that we took when we advanced last upon the Douro; this has been from the necessity imposed upon Lord W. of following the track of the Enemy. It is supposed we shall this time endeavour to cross the river at Tudela, by which means we avoid the Pisuerga, which it would be necessary to pass if we passed the Douro at Tordesillas.—Marmont is reported to have died at Arevallos. The command of the French Army is said to have devolved upon General Foy, who, if we may believe the prisoners, gained but little credit for his exertions on the battle of the 22d. He commanded the Cavalry.

31st. On the 29th we crossed the river Adaja & encamped near a village called Hornillos on the Eresma. Yesterday we passed the latter at a Ford, and the Cega at a bridge; after marching four Leagues we were directed to halt in a wood near the Village of Boccillo, for orders; this place was only distant five miles from Valladolid, the Spires of which City we could plainly see. While we were indulging ourselves with the idea of entering it, an order was received to retrograde two Leagues, & encamp on the Cega, where we remain this day.—The Enemy left Valladolid yesterday Morning. Lord Wellington with a squadron of the 11th Dragoons entered it a few hours after. He was received with loud acclamations by the Inhabitants, and after remaining there for some hours he returned to the village of Mojados near our encampment, and where his Head Quarters are at present established.—About seven hundred sick & wounded French were found in Valladolid. The enemy have taken the direction of Aranda, a town situated on the Douro, for the purpose it is supposed of uniting with the reinforcements under Joseph; it is probable they will yet make another struggle before they abandon the Capital.

Aug. 2d. Yesterday we marched three Leagues, & encamped on the same River as the preceding day ; our march this day is only two Leagues, and we are again in bivouac on the banks of the Ceja. The last few days, we have enjoyed the luxury of Trees, having marched constantly in an extensive wood ; the soil however is very sandy, & extremely painful to the Troops in marching. The weather, as may be supposed, is most oppressively hot. Our present bivouac is about two miles from an old fortified Town called Cuellar, where Head Quarters at present are.

It is uncertain whether the enemy took the direction of Burgos or Aranda, but it is reported the former ; in which case I see no reason whatever why we should not march immediately upon the Capital. There are no Troops between Madrid and us, excepting the twelve or fourteen thousand men with Joseph : these latter are said to have quitted Segovia yesterday, having previously levied a contribution of one million & a half of Dollars on the unfortunate Inhabitants.

6th. We remained in our bivouac upon the Cega till this morning, when we marched 3 leagues in the direction of Segovia. We are encamped on the River Piron, near the Village of Mudriar, and about six Leagues distant from Segovia. Our Cavalry entered that City on the day before yesterday. There does not appear any obstacle to our marching to the Capital, should such an arrangement be the intention of Lord W. The Army of Joseph is composed in great measure of Juramantados who are said to be deserting in great numbers.—The Army of Marmont has not yet recovered from its panic ; there is little or no doubt that he himself died on the 30th, & Accts. have been received of five other Generals having also died. Our wounded General Officers are doing remarkably well, as are the wounded in general. The 6th Division with Genl. Clinton remain at Cuellar for the present ; four regiments [which] lately joined the Army, & are suffering very much from sickness, are also with him ; Head Quarters have been at Cuellar the last five days, but we know not if they have moved from thence to-day or not. Cuellar is a very old Town, possessing a most spacious Castle, in which was an Armoury ; it has been however totally destroyed by the French.

7th. Our march this day was 3 Leagues. We are bivouacked near the Village of Yenques, on the river Eresma, and distant from Segovia three leagues ; it appears the Enemy have left a Garrison in the Castle there, for the reduction of which some heavy Guns are moving with us.

The Country we have reached is much more plentiful than any we have been accustomed to for a very long period of time ; Geese, Turkeys, Ducks &c. &c. are now to be procured at a reasonable price. The Costume of the Peasantry in this neighbourhood is altogether different from any I have before seen, & considerably resembles the Chinese dress. As we pass thro' the several Towns & Villages, the acclamations of the People are unbounded.

10th. On the 8th we marched near four Leagues & bivouacked at el Palacio del Rio frio, about a league from Segovia. This place takes its name from a Royal Palace built not many years since for the accomodation of the Court while hunting in this Neighbourhood ; it is an immense square building & has fifty one windows on each face ; it has nothing remarkable except the Stair Case which is very handsome and worthy of a Royal residence. On the 9th we remained in the same bivouac ; this gave us an opportunity of visiting Segovia. We were misinformed when we were told that there was a French Garrison in that city ; it having been entirely abandoned several days since by the Enemy. It is a very ancient town, and is well worthy of observation. The Castle is known to every one who has read the History of Gil Blas, as having been the place of his Confinement, when he fell into disgrace ; on one of the Apartments is marked, " Here the celebrated Gil Blas was confined." The Cathedral is a very fine building, but will not bear the test of comparison with that of Salamanca. There is also a fine Aqueduct, and amongst other curiosities we were shewn King Joseph's Apartments in the Bishop's Palace ; in his bedroom is a Table & Chair where he sat with his head leaning on the former, from whence his Ministers could not prevail upon him to go for the space of three days, after he heard of the defeat of his Army ; he quitted Segovia on the first Inst. Head Quarters were at Segovia on the 7th, & at San Ildefonso on the 8th and 9th. This latter is estimated as one of the finest Palaces in Spain.—This day we marched four Leagues, & are bivouacked near the village of Espinal. We are now only nine Leagues from the Capital ; it appears to me very probable that Lord W. purposes entering it on the 12th, being the birthday of the Prince Regent ; we have not heard that any Opposition is expected on the part of the Enemy.—The Country we have entered to-day is mountainous, & forms a pleasing contrast to the insipid flats we have so long been marching through ; the heat is in consequence infinitely less oppressive.

11th. This day we came through the celebrated Pass of the Guadarrama. The ascent to it is beautiful, but its summit was not so difficult as we had been led to expect. From the top, had the morning been clear, we should have had a distinct view of Madrid, but the haze prevented us seeing any distant object. At the Village of Guadarrama a few of us turned off for the purpose of visiting the well known Palace of the Escurial. 1 had expected so much from it, that I must confess I was greatly disappointed. The Palace itself is as far destroyed as it well could be, the enemy having entirely stripped the regal Apartments of everything that decorated them ; notwithstanding we were much gratified by our visit, the Mausoleum, the Church, and the Library, each being worthy of observation. In the former are deposited the remains of a great number of the Kings & Queens of Spain ; amongst them is the body of Charles the 5th. The Coffins are all of the finest marble in separate niches of four, one above the other : there are twelve of these Coffins still unoccupied ; the Mausoleum is called the Pantheon, and is certainly a very splendid & beautiful edifice—the Church is also particularly elegant ; the Ceiling is beautifully painted ; the subjects are Scriptural, & the Day of Judgment is the chef d' Oeuvre.— The Library is also a large painted Room ; the subjects illustrative of the different Arts & Sciences. Not a Book however remains in it ; the French with their accustomed rapacity have taken them all ; a pair of Globes, & an Orrery alone have been spared from the grasp of these merciless Robbers. By ascending a hill & looking down upon the Escurial, the form of a Gridiron in which it was built is perceived ; it was erected by Philip the 2d in commemoration of Saint Lorenzo ; who is said to have suffered Martydom by being burnt to death on that Instrument.

We are at present six leagues from Madrid, and had flattered ourselves we should have taken quiet possession of it ; it is likely however we are deceived, as while I am writing a heavy Cannonade can be distinctly heard in that direction ; there can therefore be no doubt that they yet maintain themselves in the Retiro, & from the strength of it we may have a good deal of trouble in dislodging them from it.

21st. A long period has elapsed since my last date, from my time having been too fully occupied to allow of my bringing up my Journal. The firing heard on the Evening of the 11th proceeded from a severe skirmish which took place with the Enemy about two Leagues on this side of the Capital. Genl. D'Urban with near a thousand Portuguese Cavalry was in front with a Brigade of English Horse Artillery, supported about a half League in their rear by the Brigade of Heavy German Cavalry. Towards Evening some enemy's Cavalry shewed themselves, when a slight skirmishing took place, the Enemy retiring on Madrid. At length they appeared in considerable force ; and made a disposition to charge the Portugueze; the latter instantly fled in the most shameful manner without attempting any resistance; the consequence was that the Guns were left unprotected, and three of them were taken. At the same time, from the rapid flight of the Portugueze, the Germans had not sufficient time to get under arms, before the Enemy was amongst them; the few who were prepared made three most gallant charges on an infinitely superior force, and consequently sustained a severe loss; about fifty Men & seventy Horses. This event, so unexpected, threw a general gloom over the whole Army; Lord W. was said to be more annoyed by it than by anything that had ever happened; they were the first British Guns the Enemy had taken since the commencement of the Peninsular war. Fortunately something occurred to prevent the French from keeping possession of them, as they were found the following day spiked near Madrid; they have since been put again into a state of Service.

On the 12th we bivouacked about three Leagues from Madrid, and on the same day Lord W. & Headquarters entered the Capital. Nearly the whole of the population came out to meet him, old & young, rich & poor; it was with difficulty we could get into the Town, so excessive was the joy of the People. On the 13th at daylight our Division marched towards Madrid, & bivouacked in a wood about a mile from the City, & close to the King's Country House. I was in the town about eight o'Clock, & at this time the concourse of People was immense. The approach to Madrid within two miles of it was very fine, the Town itself is the most beautiful I ever saw; there are an immense number of Palaces, & other fine houses, and the Streets are wide and well built; it far exceeds the expectations of every one.—On the Evening of the 13th the Constitution as framed by the Cortes was proclaimed; the sight was truly affecting; the Houses of the Streets through which the procession passed were ornamented with silks of various colours; & the windows filled with remarkably fine women; everything bore the appearance of the most unsophisticated Joy. At length the Constitution was proclaimed amid the acclamations of thousands, who once more respired the air of liberty, after having for more than four years endured the galling Chains of the most odious Slavery. The rejoicings continued for three days, and for the same number of nights the town was most beautifully illuminated. In the midst of all this gaiety the preparations for carrying on the operations against the Retiro were carried on with vigour. On the night of the 13th the Outworks were stormed and taken, and on the following Morning at ten o'Clock a number of Troops deemed sufficient for the purpose were selected from the 3d Division to storm the remainder of the works. Just as they were about to move off for the purpose, a flag of Truce issued from the Fort; the result of the conference, which lasted some time, was the surrendering up the Fort and all it contained to the Allied Army. The surprize excited by this most unlooked for event was so great, that it was with difficulty believed. At four o'Clock in the Afternoon the Garrison marched out with the honors of war, to the amount of two thousand; they were nearly all in a state of intoxication, and their gestures and language was very violent; they exclaimed that they were sold, and that their Officers ought every one to be burnt alive. For my own part I shall never cease to believe, that the Governor yielded to the "Auri sacra fames" tho' such an opinion is very assiduously scouted at Head Quarters; at all events it may very fairly be inferred that that Gentleman will never break his Parole.—In the Fort were found 190 pieces of Cannon, 20,000 Musquets, Ammunition in proportion, and immense Magazines of every description.

On the 18th our Division marched & bivouacked on the same ground we occupied on the 12th. On the 19th it reached the Escurial, where we still remain; I did not leave Madrid myself till the 19th and arrived here just at the same time with the Division. I will confess I never left a place with more sincere regret, having passed there a most delightful week. On the day of my arrival there I was particularly fortunate in being introduced to a Family of the first rank, and of the most amiable manners ; from them I received attentions and kindnesses I can never forget ; the father is an old General Officer, and in the time of Charles the 4th held the situation of Minister at war, and a Privy Counsellor of the Empire.

The principal curiosities of Madrid are the Royal Palace (which in point of magnificence is said to be unrivalled in Europe), the Museum, and the public walk called the Prado ; in the Palace & Museum are some Chef d'Oeuvres of Rubens, & Titian, and other great Masters, in the latter are to be found collections of every Beast, Bird, Fish, Mineral, precious Stones, &c. &c. in the world, besides an infinite variety of Curiosities from every part of the Globe. The Prado is said to be the finest public walk in Europe.—The Churches in Madrid have nothing extra-ordinary in them ; the principal one is dedicated to San Isidro, but it is very inferior to the Cathedral at Salamanca ; there are two Theatres tolerably good, but the performers are very indifferent, the principal Actors having gone off with the intrusive King. The two great inconveniences we sustained at Madrid were the excessive heat (by far greater than I have ever before experienced it) and the hardness of the pavement, so much so that there was a general complaint of sore feet.—What most particularly strikes a stranger in Madrid is the elegance of the Women, the beauty of their dress, and their inimitable walk.

There are at present concentrated in the Escurial, the 1st 4th, 5th, & 7th Divisions of Infantry, & Generals Pack's & Bradford's Brigades of Portugueze ; the 3d Division remains at Madrid, with Head Quarters ; the Light are still at Valverde, & the 6th have moved from Cuellar to Olmedo. I know not where are the Head Quarters of the Cavalry.

In the meantime the French have again occupied Valladolid & the neighbouring places, but it is not apprehended they will march upon Salamanca, as such a movement could not be performed without risk. From the extreme heat of the weather a season of rest is most devoutly to be wished, but it is very little to be expected.

24th. Nothing has occurred to induce us to expect we shall quit this place soon; Head Quarters remain in Madrid with the Light & 3d Divisions; the 1st, 4th, & 7th are here; the 5th marched Yesterday Morning to Arevallo, to be in communication with Genl. Clinton.

King Joseph, who was supposed to be going to Valencia, is said to have changed his direction, & is gone towards Aragon; it is certain there have been great disturbances in his Army between the French & Spanish troops, & much blood has been shed ; many of the Families who left Madrid in his train have returned to their houses, preferring to be tried by some Court established for the purpose to remaining with him.

Sept. 15th. On the 25th Ulto. I went to Madrid, and after being there a day or two was attacked with remittent Fever, from which I have only just recovered ; I returned yesterday to the Escorial, where my Division alone remains ; Lord W. left Madrid on the 1st inst. & took the direction of Valladolid ; he has with him the 1st, 5th, 6th, & 7th Divisions, & Genl. Pack's & Bradford's Brigades of Portugueze. It is conjectured they are by this time near Burgos, the Siege of which place, or rather of the Castle there, is determined on. By the last Accts. it was supposed the French Army would not make a stand in that neighbourhood. In the meantime the French have raised the Siege of Cadiz ; this most important event took place on the night of the 24th Ulto. It appears to have been done with much precipitation, as they left a vast quantity of stores behind them, and it is said Artillery to the Amount of fifteen hundred pieces. This movement must have been the consequence of our possession of the Capital, by which the communication between the Armies of Soult & Suchet was threatened. By the last Accts. Soult had arrived at Granada, on his way, it was supposed, to Valencia. On the whole, everything goes on most prosperously, & it is not too much to expect that before Christmas there will not be a Frenchman on this side of the Ebro.

The weather has lately been hot beyond all precedent, but, heavy rain having set in the last few days, the temperature has become much milder.

23d. We still remain at the Escorial ; Head Quarters are at Burgos, & the Siege of the Castle at that place has commenced ; we do not know the amount of the Force the Enemy has left there; this place is wretchedly stupid, & we are entirely out of the way of all news. Genl. Hill is said to be at Talavera.

28th. It appears that on the 19th at Night a strong Outwork at Burgos was stormed ; our People were repulsed the first attack, but succeeded on the second ; our loss was severe amounting to about four hundred & fifty killed & wounded; the Fort was garrisoned by five hundred of the Enemy, of which number only seventy remain who were not bayonetted. On the Evening of the 22d a second Outwork was stormed, but without success ; the loss was not very great ; Majr. Laurie of the 79th was killed on the occasion. Genl. Hill's Corps is at Toledo & Aranjuez.

[Oct.] Octr. 6th. Another unsuccessful attack was made at Burgos on the Evening of the 29th, and, as is said, under circumstances not at all creditable to the assailants. After the very distinguished proofs of gallantry performed by the British Army in the Peninsula, it is painful to have to record these several failures, which only required the accustomed Spirit of a British Soldier to have ensured their success.

I write this at Madrid, to which place I came on the 2d Inst. I had yesterday an opportunity of witnessing a Bull fight, a spectacle the most delightful there can be to the people of this Nation, but which to a mind tinctured with the smallest degree of humanity cannot be witnessed without horror. On these occasions ten or twelve Bulls & nearly as many horses are sacrificed amid every species of cruelty, & the applauding shouts of an immense Multitude. So concordant is this Spectacle with the ideas of the Spaniards of both Sexes, that many a poor Family, who know not where to get money to purchase a bit of bread to eat, will sell the Clothes they wear, or the Bed they lie on, in order to procure wherewithal to pay for their admittance. The shouts of applause are in an exact ratio with the degrees of cruelty that are practised, and if the unfortunate Bulls are killed without half a dozen Horses & at least one of the Fighters being also Victims the disappointment is extreme. The mode of fighting is as follows :— The Animals having for several days previous been goaded by every species of torture into madness are on the day appointed let loose one by one into the Court ; two Men on Horseback and ten or twelve on Foot then commence the attack ; the former are armed with Spears, and the latter carry a large Cloth in one hand and a dart in the other. On being attacked by the Bull, they throw the cloth over his Eyes, & plunge the dart into his Body. When charged furiously by the Animal, with amazing agility they leap the fence that separates the Court from the Spectators. When the Horse is charged by the Bull, his attack is generally parried by the adroitness of the Rider, who wards it off by plunging the Spear into the Animal. It frequently happens however that the Horse receives the whole vengeance of the Bull, and tho' completely gored even to the protrusion of his Bowels, the Rider is compelled to remain on his Back till he drops. At other times the Horse & his Rider are both knocked over by the strength of the Bull, when, to prevent the Man being killed by the enraged Animal, he is assailed by all the Combatants on foot, on whom he immediately turns, and the Rider again springs into his Seat. At length the poor Animal opposed to such a host of Enemies becomes dispirited, & refuses to combat any longer, when by a refinement of cruelty the darts are armed with crackers and a great number of them are plunged into him ; the united powers of agony & terror stimulate him again into madness, but by the violence of his fury he is soon exhausted. A new personage then presents himself called the Matador, splendidly dressed, and holding in his right hand a long straight sword, and in his left a red Flag ; he advances boldly to the Animal, & placing himself immediately in front of him, by every irritating gesture at length provokes him to a momentary fury. The Bull makes a charge upon the Matador, who with an extraordinary address plunges the Sword into the Spine of the Animal, & kills him in an instant, amid the tumultous shouts of an applauding Audience. Bands of Music instantly commence playing, & three or four mules richly caparisoned are brought in, to which the carcase of the Animal is attached, and they carry it off in the galop. Another Victim is then immediately driven in, and the same scene of barbarity ensues. Though the number of Bulls for yesterday's Amusement was ten, I could not witness the sufferings of more than one ; I had a presentiment of the disgust I should experience, and I can with truth assert that my feeling was never before so completely horrified. The endurance of this barbarous amusement, and the protection afforded to it by the Government, I consider as a stain upon the National Character, but the applause & joy manifested by the people at the sufferings of the poor Animals has given me an idea of their hearts as bad as it is possible to conceive. It is to the credit of the English Character, that scarcely a British Officer has gone to witness it a second time.

Genl. Hill is here at present, and in addition to his Corps has taken under his command the Light 3d & 4th Divisions ; the latter is coming from the Escorial into this Neighbourhood ; this change is said to be in consequence of some movements of Soult who appears to be threatening the Capital.

13th. I quitted Madrid yesterday & found my Brigade at Pinto, a large village distant three leagues from the Capital. The demonstrations of Soult were the means of making Genl. Hill concentrate his force ; at present, it is supposed, that Soult has taken a direction towards Valencia for the purpose of concentrating with Suchet.—Burgos still resists all our efforts ; the Outworks however at length have been all carried, and nothing remains but the Castle. The Enemy made a Sally a few Evenings since upon our Trenches, & were immediately driven in ; in a short time they sallied a second time with an increased force, and succeeded in driving our People from their work; and, before the Covering Parties could repel them, they had knocked off the Trannions of one of the only heavy guns we have there ; in this last Service Majr. Cocks of the 79th, an Officer of very great promise, was unfortunately killed ; it is said our total loss since the commencement of the Siege amounts to fourteen hundred men. Lord Wellington is expected at Madrid as soon as Genl. Paget shall have arrived at Burgos to take the command of that part of the Army.

25th. Since my last date, having been Gazetted to a Staff Surgeoncy, I am at present at Madrid waiting the result of an application of Genl. Cole, who has written to the Inspr.of Hospls. to request I may be appointed to this Division; should it fail, I shall go immediately to Burgos. On the 23d I bade adieu to the 40th Regiment, after having been with them nearly eleven years ; they are unquestionably one of the finest Regiments in the Army, and will always have my warmest wishes for their welfare.

On the 21st the 4th Division moved from Valdemoro & Pinto to Villages near Aranjuez, and the 3d Divn. marched the same day to occupy the quarters vacated by the 4th Divn. On the 22d I rode over to Aranjuez, which has ever been esteemed the favorite Royal residence in this Country. The Palace is by no means equal in point of magnificence to that at this place ; it stands immediately on the Tagus ; the gardens have been very beautiful & tasty, but latterly have been suffered to run to decay. The chief curiosity at Aranjuez is a small royal residence called the Casa del Labrador ; it is exquisitely beautiful. The day I was at Aranjuez there was an unusual bustle ; the Enemy in front were making demonstrations of advancing on that Road, & on our part every precaution was making ; all the heavy Baggage, Forge & Forage Waggons &c. &c. were moving to the rear for the purpose of crossing the River, and the several Bridges were mined and ready to be blown up. On the following day however it was ascertained they had taken a direction to their right ; had they come on by the Aranjuez Road, they would have had to encounter a most superb position, which, I doubt not, would have proved to them another Busaco ; it is situated about five Leagues from hence, & two from Aranjuez. This Morning it is said our Troops are again all in Motion in the direction of Alcala, which is to our left, as the Movements of the Enemy indicate an intention of endeavouring to penetrate to the Capital, by the road of Guadalaxara. The intrusive King is said to have reached Cuenca, which looks as though he had really hopes of again possessing himself of this place. In the midst of all these movements it is a subject of much regret that, in the event of a general Action here, there is no certainty of our having Lord W. to preside over it. Our last Accts. from Burgos are to the 20th. It appears that on the evening of the 19th another unsuccessful attempt was made to storm ; on the 20th the Enemy shewed every disposition to advance & relieve the place ; Massena had assumed the command ; Lord W. withdrew all the Troops from before Burgos, with the exception of the First Divisn. & was determined to give Battle if the Enemy offered it ; under all these circumstances much & very important matter may be expected to take place in a few days ; there is some little panic here, but it is not general ; one Portugueze regiment only is left at this place.

28th. The Enemy are in force at Aranjuez, but it is not known that they have as yet passed the Tagus, though the Fords are all practicable. A general Action is expected in a day or two, and nothing is heard of Lord W. The Spaniards in particular are in despair on the occasion, & augur nothing but defeat from his absence ; it is yet to be hoped he may arrive in time.

The Enemy made a strong reconnoisance in front of Burgos, with fifteen Squadrons of Cavalry & about ten thousand Infantry ; Lord W. attacked them & immediately repulsed them with loss. Since that he has entirely raised the siege, & our army is said to be in position about two Leagues on this side of Burgos.

[Nov.]

Novr. 1. The events of the last few days have been of the most painful nature, nor were they at all suspected by any one. On the 29th rumours were afloat in the Morning, that the British Army was about to retreat for the purpose of concentrating with Lord W. Towards the Afternoon an unusual bustle was observed to prevail among the Civil Authorities & their Families, & Equipages were seen severally quitting the Town. On the morning of the 30th the removal of all the sick & wounded and the destruction of the Guns in the Retiro left no sort of doubt that we were going to abandon the Capital ; the Shops were nearly all shut, & the greatest agitation evidently prevailed.—I quitted Madrid myself in the Afternoon of the 30th, having previously taken leave of the Family I have before spoken of and for whom I must ever entertain the most grateful recollection. Their situation is peculiarly a painful one ; the state of health of the old general entirely precludes his being removed, & from the Family having been always suspected during the time the Enemy were in Madrid before, & their having given constant proof during our stay of their attachment to the British, they will, I fear, have to undergo many hardships & indignities. The most profound grief pervaded them when I bade them adieu, & I can with truth say I participated most warmly in their distresses.

On the night of the 30th I remained with a part of the Army in Las Rosas, about two & a half Leagues on the Road leading to the Escorial. On that night the Retiro was entirely & most effectually blown up without at all injuring the Town, which was at one time feared would be the case. At Las Rosas I learned from Genl. Pakenham, that the enemy had been secretly able to collect such a force in the North, that there was every reason to fear they would overwhelm Lord W. if brought to action, or otherwise press him so hard as to prevent our forming a junction with him. Yesterday I accompanied Genl. P. to the Escorial, & here we learned that there was every reason to believe that the enemy had occupied the strong Pass of the Guadarrama, & that there was no retreat for us but by the Mountains of Avila, by which it was considered our Sick, Artillery, Stores & Baggage would be all lost ; Lord W. was supposed to have been worsted in a general Action, & to have been compelled to retire beyond the Tormes ; in short nothing could possibly be more gloomy than our prospects. In the evening Genl. Hill arrived here, & we found that he was in possession of a letter from Lord W. of the 29th & that everything was going on pretty well. The rumour of the French having occupied the Pass proved to be unfounded, nor is there any fear of such an event. It is still supposed probable that, in order to join Lord W., Genl. Hill will be compelled to attack the French Army in his front, unless they decline such a contest by suffering the two Armies quietly to unite. The Enemy had not entered Madrid at a late hour last Night, but it is supposed they are there by this. Head Quarters of Sir R. Hill remain here to-day, & it is probable we shall cross the Guadarrama to-morrow. In the meantime Soult by no means presses us as might be expected from his superiority of Cavalry ; there has been but little skirmishing hitherto ; the day before yesterday, they attempted to force a

[1812]
[Nov].
Bridge defended by our People, and tho' they attacked it in very superior numbers they were driven back with loss, notwithstanding it is said their Officers made most extraordinary exertions to animate their men—In the North there was a sharp affair in which we sustained a severe loss it is said in Cavalry, particularly the 16th Dragoons ; the enemy's Cavalry came on in a manner perfectly wild, & from their numbers drove our People before them ; they were at length however checked by the German Light Infantry.

It is impossible to calculate the consequences of our being compelled to quit the Capital, but it is not unlikely that it will have so great an effect on the minds of the People as to excite a despondency fatal to the liberties of the Country. It is certain that they have not availed themselves as they should have done of the much that has been done, & it may I think be fairly questioned whether in that time, with two thirds of their country unoccupied by the French, they have added ten thousand Men to their Army.

3d. I moved yesterday morning with the Head Quarters of Sir R. Hill from the Escorial ; we crossed the Guadarrama & halted at the village of Espinar. This morning we marched five Leagues, and are now at a place called Lavajos. Lord Wellington is at Rueda, & the probability that we could not effect a junction with him without an action is now at end ; our Force may now be said to have joined him, at least tomorrow such will be the case.—The enemy did not arrive at Madrid till the night before last ; they approached it very cautiously with a small party of Dragoons, &, having ascertained that we had entirely left it, they demanded the Keys, & having ordered forty thousand Rations for three days they quitted it, & proceeded to Valdemoro, where they were in force. It is not known whether they have since returned to it, but there is a very general idea that they do not mean to occupy it, but that the present movements of Soult indicate an intention of proceeding down the Valley of the Tagus, &

making an incursion into the Alemtejo : such a manoeuvre would oblige Lord W. to detach an opposing force & prevent him from pressing on the Army of the North.—On reaching the Guadarrama Pass, the whole of the Cavalry made a forced March, & now precede the Infantry, they not being required in the Country we are passing thro'. Indeed it does not appear that the Enemy are sending a man after us.

6th. On the 4th we marched to a village called Villa Nueva de Gomez, and received intelligence in the Afternoon that the Advanced Guard of the Enemy had reached Villa Castin, a place about five Leagues distant. Yesterday we halted at Fontiveros, four Leagues; the Enemy followed us, & remained two Leagues from Sir R. Hill's Head Quarters; a few Shots were in the course of the day exchanged.

I quitted Fontiveros this morning at daybreak and am at present at Peñaranda, three Leagues distant. I have not heard what are the movements of the Enemy this day; Sir R. Hill, it is intended, shall have his Hd. Quarters about half a league from hence in front, and with him will remain the Light & 4th Divisions as the rear guard. The weather is not promising, and it has rained a good deal to-day; should it continue it will very much embarrass our movements. The numbers of Sick & the quantity of Baggage and Stores is so immense that they appear to have no end. To cover these the Army has been obliged to make only a short march of only two leagues & a half to-day. This place is four Leagues from the Tormes, which River it is probable the Sick, Stores, & Baggage, will all cross to-morrow. Lord W. remained yesterday morning at Rueda but it is said he has moved.—Every one is ignorant of the intentions of his Lordship, but it is supposed, should Soult follow us with all his force, that his superiority in numbers will be so great as to render the issue of a general Action too hazardous to be risked; in which case nothing appears to remain for us but to retire once more behind the Agueda; the mere possibility of such an event is mortifying in the extreme.

8th. Yesterday morning we marched to Alba de Tormes, and the whole day was occupied in passing over the Bridge the Sick, Baggage, Stores, &c. &c. Most fortunately the enemy did not press us or the consequences must have been either to abandon them, or otherwise, an Action to cover them. In the Evening the 2d Division crossed the River, & bivouacked on the opposite side; the Baggage continued to pass the whole Night & this Morning the 3d, 4th, & Light Divisions crossed, as also the Cavalry, the Enemy shewing no disposition to come after us. Genl. Hill had given directions that his Head Quarters should be this Evening at Calvaraia, a village midway between Alba & Salamanca, but about midday this arrangement was altered, & he determined on remaining here this Night; the 2d & Portugueze Divisions, with the Brigade of Cavalry that accompanied them from the Alemtejo, recrossed the river and are cantoned here. It is said the enemy are in Peñaranda, but I know not whether they are there in force or not; strong picquets of Cavalry & Infantry are gone out on that Road. Hopes are revived in consequence of the 3d, 4th, & Light Divisions having marched to join Lord W. at Salamanca, that it is his intention to defend the City; a very short time must show what is his policy, as the weather has set in so very bad that it will be altogether impossible to keep the Field many days.

11th. On the 9th I quitted Alba, & repaired to Salamanca where I received orders to join the 4th Division as Staff Surgeon; on that day nothing particular occurred. Yesterday Morning the Light Division marched into Salamanca, where they were cantoned with the 7th. The 1st, 5th, and 6th were in Position in front of the Town, on the same ground we occupied during the Siege of the Forts at that place; the 3d & 4th remained in bivouack midway between Alba & Salamanca near to Calvaraia de Amiba, and Genl. Hill at

Calvaraia de Baxo with his force with the exception of Genl.
Howard's Brigade, who remained in Alba for its defence.
Towards the Evening the Enemy in force attempted to dislodge
our People from that Town, but failed; we lost about forty
men on the occasion. There has been some fire in the same
place this Morning, but the result is not known; early to-day
also there was a good deal of Musquetry near the Ford of
Huerta, which is defended by Genl. Pack; of the issue of this
we are likewise ignorant; neither is it known that there has
been any change in the Positions of the different Divisions
since yesterday; Lord W. has his Headquarters at Salamanca,
& it would appear that it is his intention to defend the place.
The weather is again very fine, and the River will soon be
fordable in many places; this may give a new turn to the
movements of the Enemy.

14th. 5 a.m. There has been nothing done since the
11th, when the Enemy again attempted to get possession of
Alba, & at the same time to dislodge Genl. Pack from the
Ford at Huerta; in both which attempts they failed. On the
12th everything was remarkably quiet, & yesterday not a shot
was exchanged, but their movements during the Afternoon
& Evening indicate every probability that there will be an
Action this day. They reconnoitred & tried several of the
Fords & moved a considerable force upon two or three of
them. In consequence we are all upon the alert; it wants
but an hour of daybreak, when the intentions of the Enemy
will probably be manifested; it is impossible they can remain
long inactive; the want of Provisions will compel them either
to fight or retire. Their force is not exactly ascertained, but
it is conjectured to amount to seventy thousand men; Joseph
is said to be with them.

26th. At Day break on the 14th the Enemy crossed the
Tormes above Alba; they passed considerable bodies of
Cavalry with some Artillery & Infantry; about 8 a.m. the
bridge at Alba was blown up. The 4th Division had taken

up before daylight a position on some heights above that Town to cover the retreat of Genl. Howard's Brigade from it; this done the army retired near a League & took up its position. The Troops in position on this side of the River consisted of the Light 2d, 3d, & 4th Divisions. The intentions of the Enemy very soon manifested themselves; they moved with rapidity to their left; some skirmishing took place, but before the Evening our right flank was completely turned. Immediately after dusk, the Army was again in motion, we retrograded another League, and a position was taken up upon the Arapiles, the same heights where the battle of the 22d July was fought; Lord W. had this time the advantage of being able to take possession of both Hills; our left, which was formed by the 4th Division, rested on the village of Calvaraia di Amiba. All this day the enemy continued to move across the river immense Columns of Infantry.

On the 15th it was very soon evident that the Enemy declined attacking us in position ; he pursued the same system as the preceding day, and moved to his left. Lord W. was therefore compelled to withdraw the several Divisions from the other side of the Water, & abandon Salamanca to its fate. To prevent the enemy getting possession of the high road leading to Ciudad Rodrigo, the position of the Arapiles was also abandoned, and the whole Army moved upon that Road. About noon it commenced raining in torrents, which did not cease during the whole Afternoon & Evening ; the Army bivouacked about two Leagues from Salamanca on the Ciudad Rodrigo Road.—The Morning of the 16th was equally wet, but it cleared in the course of the day ; the Army marched in two Columns ; we were in the left Column, & had the Rear Guard, we marched three leagues, & halted in a wood near the Village of Martilla. We were not annoyed by the Enemy during our march, but we had scarcely been an hour upon our ground when they shewed themselves upon some heights, & also in a place about a Mile in our front ; the 2d Divn. on our right skirmished with them ; fortunately they had not any Artillery up, & we therefore passed the Evening quietly.

At 4 o'clock on the morning of the 17th we continued our retreat ; the weather was again dreadful, & the roads in consequence scarcely passable ; after marching three leagues we halted near the Village of San Muñoz, at which place there is a Ford over a River ; the object of our halt was to cover the retreat of Baggage & Stragglers, as also the rear of the right Column, which had to pass at this Ford. The Enemy pressed us a good deal at this place, & brought up about twenty pieces of Artillery on some heights opposite to us. There was some severe skirmishing during the Afternoon, in which we lost some Officers & about an hundred & fifty Men ; but we had this day particularly to lament the loss of Sir Edw. Paget who very recently came out to this Country as second in Command ; he was passing from one Divn. to another, unconscious of any danger, when a party of French Dragoons surprised him & carried him off ; they also possessed themselves of a great deal of Baggage, & amongst others the whole of the Baggage of Lord Dalhousie lately arrived, was taken. After everything had crossed the Ford, we marched half a league, & bivouacked for the night near the village of Abrillas : the rain continued so heavy that we were literally up to our Ancles in Mud & Water.—On the 18th the weather was better ; our march this day was four leagues & a half ; we halted on the side of a Hill half a League on this side the Village of Tenebron. Most fortunately for the 4th Division the enemy did not press us this day, or we must have suffered dreadfully from their Artillery ; we had to wait on the top of a Hill several hours, to cover the retreat of other Divisions who cut in upon us, and from this Hill had the Enemy pursued us they would have had the finest opportunity in the world of annoying us, as after descending it we had an extensive plain to cross, which for two miles would have been completely within the range of their Artillery.—On the 19th we marched only a League and a half and bivouacked in a Wood one League from Ciudad Rodrigo, at which place Head Quarters had arrived the preceding Day. There was no small degree of consternation prevailing there, from the circumstance of the breach (which had been entirely repaired) having given way from the violence of the late rains. The people were however soon tranquilized on finding that the Enemy were ceasing to follow us ; in fact they were as completely exhausted as ourselves and in consequence incapable of further annoying us.—On the 20th the Rains again commenced with all their former violence ; the march of the Divn. was this Day a most painful one, four Leagues & a half through almost impassable Roads : we bivouacked on the very same ground that we were on on the 10th [of] June last, when the Army was concentrating for the purpose of proceeding against Salamanca.—On the 21st we went into Cantonments, the Head Quarters of the Division being at Villa de Ciervo, the same place they were in on the 21st November last. These Cantonments however are considered merely temporary, it being understood that we shall proceed in a few days to occupy winter Cantonments in the direction of the Douro for the purpose of being nearer our supplies.— On reviewing the late retreat there is certainly cause of much mortification. After so splendid a campaign results more brilliant were doubtlessly expected ; at the same time it is but fair to take the whole campaign, and not look only to the last two months as is the case with many ; if the question is fairly put, what has Lord W. done this campaign ? the answer as fairly is ; he has secured the two keys of Portugal ; raised the siege of Cadiz, cleared the South of Spain ; destroyed the French Magazines at Madrid, and fed his army five months on those supplies which otherwise would have been possessed by the Enemy. In point of what is called military luck Lord W. has lately not had his usual good fortune ; had the rains when we were at Madrid set in two days earlier, the Enemy could not have crossed the Tagus, & thus the junction of their Armies would have been prevented ; again had they commenced two days sooner than they did at Salamanca, they could not have passed the Tormes, and instead of having that

River for their line they must of necessity have retrograded as far as the Domo. Every effort was made by his Lordship to save Salamanca, but such is the nature of the Positions on this side of the River that an Enemy with a superior force can at all times turn them. Lord W. calculates the force opposed to him, consisting of the united Armies of Joseph, Marmont & Soult at an hundred thousand Men ; their Cavalry alone amounted to eight thousand ; ours can scarcely be estimated at five thousand. It may not be irrevelant here to notice the melancholy falling off from that dash & spirit which formerly distinguished our Cavalry ; this lamentable dereliction from what they were is not attributed to any degeneracy in the Men, but to the incapacity, not to add, want of courage, of many of their Generals. I have long forborne to notice this circumstance ; but it has become so notorious, that there is scarcely a Dinner party, or assemblage of persons where military matters are at all discussed, where the conduct of our Cavalry Generals is not spoken of with disgust & contempt.

The late retreat will long be remembered for its excessive severity ; if I mistake not the Gazettes will in a short time be abundantly productive of resignations in consequence of it. There are various opinions as to the amount of the loss the allied Army sustained in the retreat, but I think myself it may very fairly be estimated at two thousand. Many of these perished on the road from the excessive severity of the weather : of those picked up by the Enemy a good many may be expected to escape.

Head Quarters of the Army moved on the 24th from Ciudad Rodrigo to their old station at Frenada, and there it is probable they will remain during the Winter. If we are quite three or four Months in Quarters, the Army will again become respectable in point of numbers. It is rumoured that it is the intention of Ministers to send every Man they can muster to this country and, if affairs continue to go on well in Russia, we shall I trust

[1812]
[Nov.] next Year be in a state to commence another brilliant Campaign, & which in its consequences, will prove more fortunate than the one we have just concluded. The Enemy are not nearer to us than Salamanca, & it appears that Joseph, not willing to trust himself with the good people of Madrid, has for the present established his Court at Valladolid.—The weather has set in frosty, & promises to be fine for some time.

[DEC.] Decr. 4th. On the Evening of the 26th our Route arrived, and on the morning of the 27th we commenced our march for our old Cantonment, San João de Pesqueira; our route lay as follows :—

27th.	Junca.
28th.	Azinhal.
29th.	Laminas.
30th.	Sant' Euphemia.
Dec. 1st.	Manilva.
2nd.	Sedevin.
3rd.	San João de Pesqueira.

Nothing could be more miserable than our accommodation during the whole march, and even here at Pesqueira we are anything but comfortable, tho' only one Regiment is here with the Headquarters of the Divn. It is probable we shall remain at least a period of three Months, & under that presumption Chimnies are building in all the Houses, where it is possible to persuade the owners of them to add this species of Comfort, a case frequently of great difficulty. It is to be understood that the expence attending the building of a Fireplace is always paid by the Officer; five times out of six the Chimnies are destroyed by the owners of the Houses immediately on our quitting them.

17th. This place affords no matter for a Journal; it has rained incessantly ever since we have been here nor is there any prospect of better weather.

Lord W. is gone to Cadiz to consult with the Regency as is supposed in his Capacity of Generalissimo, the plan of the next Campaign, & enforce by his presence the adoption of such preparations as in the meantime may be requisite.

It appears that the Enemy only remained four days in Madrid ; they abandoned it on the 6th Ulto. & had not again occupied it on the 25th. There is reason however to believe that they have since entered it.

Jan. 5th. The Enemy reoccupied Madrid on the 3d Ulto. but, from the complexion of affairs in the North, there is every reason to hope that in a very short time they will feel themselves obliged to withdraw their Army from the Peninsula ; four thousand Cavalry have already gone to France.

Lord W. arrived at Cadiz on the 24th Ulto. and is to return via Lisbon, where great preparations are making for his reception and where he is idolized as little less than a Divinity.

The frost set in here on Christmas Day, and has continued more or less ever since ; there appears little difference in the Climate here and in England ; the only advantage here is that at midday there is more Sun.

12th. Already the successes of the Russians begin to appear in this Country ; the Enemy have abandoned the line of the Tormes and we hear they are mining Burgos and preparing again to evacuate the Capital ; it is confidently said they have commenced defiling a large body of Infantry to France. Lord W. is expected at Hd. Qrs. on the 17th.

February 1st. Lord W. arrived at Frenada on the 25th. Nothing respecting the object of his journey to Cadiz has transpired, but whatever it may have been, it is said his wishes have not been realized by the Regency at Cadiz.

The Enemy it appears still occupy the Tormes, but in less force ; various accounts from Spain make it appear probable that they have it in contemplation to retire beyond the Ebro.

The Weather continues very cold, and the number of sick is still considerable ; the Army is yet very far from being in a state to take the Field. It is probable we shall not move from our Cantonments for at least these two Months.

[1813]
[Feb.] 14th. I left Pesqueira on the 2d for Lamego, where I arrived on the 4th, & where I still remain, being on Evidence on a General Court Martial sitting on Lieut. Colonel Archdale, 40th Regiment.—Lamego is a Town of considerable Population, situated near the Douro, & is a Bishop's See; I am quartered in his Palace; he is a very unostentatious old man, but is said to be the most charitable Man alive; so greatly is he venerated that it is reported, on his death, he will be canonized.

The Cathedral is handsome, but the same levity I have observed amongst the Priests in other places prevails here also.

Notwithstanding the entire destruction of the French Army in the North, it does not appear that the Enemy have as yet commenced any retrograde movements. It will indeed be extraordinary if they maintain their present ground during the ensuing Campaign.

25th. The Court Martial did not terminate till the 22d, on which day I quitted Lamego, & arrived at Pesqueira yesterday.

The worthy old Bishop & myself became extremely intimate during my stay at his house; he possesses many virtues, but is extremely bigoted; he assured me of his entire belief in the near fulfilment of a Prophecy, which states that about this time the whole world will be brought over to the true faith, which faith of course in his idea is the Catholic.

This day I give over all the Papers relating to my Situation in the Division to a Gentleman appointed to succeed me.—By the unsolicited kindness of Dr. McGregor I have leave of absence from the 4th Inst. for two Months to England; I will not here attempt to describe the thousand fond feelings the anticipation of revisiting that land of happiness is calculated to arouse in every breast possessed of common Sensibility; they are indeed inexplicable.

March 2d. On the 26th Ulto. I quitted Pesqueira, Genl. Cole having the day before received an order to have the Divn. in readiness to march. I remained that night at Sedevin with my old Friends of the 40th. The following Day I rode four Leagues to a Village called Villar where I remained with my Friend Col. Carr of the 83d ; before leaving Sedevin, they were apprized that the Division was to march on the 28th, but they were ignorant of their destination, tho' it was supposed to be the Neighbourhood of the Coa or Agueda. On the 28th my route was to Pedrosos, five Leagues ; and on the 6th March I reached Vizeu, three leagues. Vizeu is a large Town and is a Bishop's See ; the Cathedral has nothing in it worthy of Notice ; the Town is not at present occupied by Troops but is a General Hospl. Station, containing about twelve hundred Sick ; the Guards in Vizeu & the neighbourhood have in the last two or three months lost six hundred men by sickness.—This morning I quitted Vizeu, and came to a large village called Tondella, three Leagues through a beautiful Country ; the Weather set in fine the day I left Pesqueira, & has continued delightful ever since.

6th. On the 3d my route was four Leagues to a Village called Mortiagoa where I was well accommodated in the house of the Padre Prior of the place.—On the 4th another four Leagues to a village called Mealhada ; this day I passed over the Sierra of Busaco where the Action was fought in September 1810 ; the unburied Bones of the French still point out the place of Combat, & will remain an everlasting Monument of the rashness of their Commander. Yesterday I reached Coimbra, three Leagues. This place has suffered very little from the incursion of the French ; it is the third Town in Portugal and has a very fine Cathedral, which however is not well finished. Notwithstanding it is so large a Town there is a greater difficulty in procuring a Billet in it, than any other Town in the Country, though the people have suffered less almost than any other ; I look upon them as the most uncivil in Portugal, perhaps with the exception of those of Lisbon.

This day I have only come two Leagues, to a town called Condeixa formerly one of the prettiest in Portugal, but which now exhibits a memorable instance of French barbarity, scarcely a single house remaining ; when I last passed thro' it, it was in flames.

8th. Yesterday I halted at Pombal, & this day at Leyria. Both places are nearly a heap of Ruins, but are beginning somewhat to recover themselves. The Cathedral here is undergoing repair as fast as circumstances will admit ; it was only half destroyed ; the walls only of the Bishop's Palace are remaining ; but he lives here notwithstanding in a small house.—The horrors the Enemy committed especially on this Road are not without their use ; the sight of them have had their due effect upon the minds of the Portugueze Soldiery ; & it is I verily believe a holy thirst of vengeance which keeps them to their Colours ; for were it not with them a war of feeling it would be idle to suppose they would remain consolidated with the miserable Pay & feeding they receive.—The weather continues delightfully fine, but the heat already for three or four hours in the Day is becoming oppressive.

27th. The long interval since my last has been occasioned by illness; on the 9th I proceeded to a small Inn, four Leagues, where I got tolerably well accommodated.—On the 10th I set off for Alcoentre, six Leagues ; on reaching Rio Mayor, four Leagues, I felt myself extremely unwell with the usual Symptoms of Fever ; notwithstanding I proceeded on my journey, & reached Alcoentre, where I was obliged to go immediately to Bed.—The following Morning (11th) feeling a little better, I mounted my Horse, & with some difficulty reached Villa Franca on the Tagus, & distant from Lisbon five Leagues. In the Evening of the same I availed myself of a Boat going down to Lisbon, & arrived at Lisbon that night at half past Eleven, extremely ill ; where with the utmost difficulty I succeeded in procuring a Bed. The next day (12th) I made several ineffectual attempts to procure a

Billet, & was shocked at the pitiful evasions made at the several houses at which I presented my Billets. It appeared to me there was a degree of ingratitude in their conduct (considering it is to the British they are indebted that the French do not at this moment occupy Lisbon) which ought to be held up to everlasting execration, not because it happened to myself, but as it is notorious that a sick Officer constantly finds the same difficulty in Lisbon in making good his Billet. At length, in a state of absolute exhaustion from fatigue, I had the good fortune to meet a most particular friend in the Person of a Mr. Guthrie, at the Head of the Medical Department here, who immediately brought me to his house & had a comfortable Bed prepared for me, from which I did not rise till the 24th.—My disease was the Bilious Remittent Fever of the country, and I feel it is owing to the unremitting attention & judicious treatment of Mr. G. that I am indebted to my early recovery from a Complaint which was ushered in in its attack by Symptoms of peculiar violence.

I am now convalescent, & tho' in a state of great debility, shall I doubt not speedily regain my wonted strength. In the meantime my delay at the Court Martial at Lamego, Journey down, & subsequent illness have together spun out my leave to within one week of its termination; I feel I shall not be able to embark before its expiration and to [do] it afterwards without a further extension would be an act of manifest impropriety. I have therefore this day written to Hd. Quarters on the subject, and I cannot for a moment bring myself to doubt that by any possibility a further indulgence will be denied me.—I therefore still fondly anticipate being in England by the 20th of the ensuing Month.

[APR.] April 9th. On the 28th Ulto. at Night I had the misfortune to experience a relapse, and tho' short in duration my Fever was scarcely less violent than the preceding One; I have now been several days Convalescent, & the two last days have been able to ride out on Horseback; notwithstanding, I regain my strength very slowly—My leave to England is now beyond the caprice of any individual, a Medical Board having recommended me there for the recovery of health.—A convoy is expected to sail about the 14th, and with it, God willing, I hope to take my passage to that land where all my wishes centre.

25th. After making every arrangement to go home in a transport, an offer of a passage in the Impeteux of 78 Guns (the Convoying Ship) was made me, & I accordingly embarked in her on the 17th at Night. On the Morning of the 18th we got under weigh with near sixty sail, and in the course of the day entirely lost sight of Lisbon. Notwithstanding that it is certainly a handsome City, I dislike it more than any place I was ever in, and this altogether from the want of cleanliness of its Inhabitants.—The last few days I was there afforded me an opportunity of witnessing their most splendid processions, & Church services (it being Passion week) ; some of the Music was really beautiful, being entirely executed by public Performers.

Since we have been at sea, we have been almost constantly baffled by contrary winds ; we are now out a week, and are only this day in Lat. 40. 29. Our prospect is however at present better, as we are now very nearly able to lie on our course.—Our Mess in the Ward room consists of twenty four, & much good humour prevails ; the monotony of the Passage is a good deal relieved by the bustle that always exists in a Ship of this size.—We have had a good deal of hard blowing with a high running sea, but hitherto I have not at all suffered from sea-sickness.—The day after quitting the Tagus, we fell in with the Pomona, having Sir Thos. Graham, & other General Officers on board for the Army under Lord W.— The Impeteux is commanded by a Captain Bateman who to much professional knowledge adds a temper of the most conciliatory nature, & is much beloved by his Officers. The latter are particularly civil to all their Guests; indeed the perfect harmony subsisting between them & the Military on board evinces how entirely the two professions are qualified to esteem each the other.

[MAY] May 3d. We this morning at daylight made Scilly, & as the wind appears likely to blow for some time from the Eastward, the Commodore has determined upon that Anchorage, till a change takes place; this is a severe disappointment to all as we may be detained there a very long time; as we are at present to leeward of the Roadstead, it is uncertain whether we shall be able to get in to-day.

7th. We anchored late on the 3d in St Mary's Roadstead. On the following Morning, the Wind being fair, signal was again made to weigh; we had time however to go ashore, and visit the Capital of the Scilly Islands; it is rather [a] pretty place, & the neatness & cleanliness of the Houses could not fail to strike a Person who had lived near four years in the Peninsula.

We were scarcely out of the Roadstead, when the Wind again shifted to the Eastward, and we have since been beating about the Channel; we are at present off Plymouth, & the wind being at South, we are just enabled to lie our Course: there is however little of it.—We may possibly reach Spithead to-morrow, but our passage hitherto has been so unfortunate, that I am afraid to hope such will be the case; had we not had Convoy with us, we should have been at the end of our passage upwards of a week since. Notwithstanding the many advantages a Man of War possesses over a Transport I will confess that my Philosophy was never put to such severe trials as it has been the last few days—What sickness so painful, as that sickness of the heart which ariseth from hope deferred.

CHARLES BOUTFLOWER
(F.R.C.S.)

was the fourth son of the Reverend John Boutflower, Vicar of Seamer, Yorkshire, his mother being Susanna, daughter of Samuel Peach, of Chalford, Gloucestershire. He was born at Enfield, Middlesex, 2 February, 1782, and received his training for the medical profession from his eldest brother, Mr. John Johnson Boutflower of Manchester, and at the University of Edinburgh. At the close of the year 1801, he joined the 40th Regiment, then at Malta, as an assistant Surgeon. He served with his Regiment in the West Indies and South America, and afterwards during the Peninsula War, obtaining promotion as Surgeon to the staff of Sir Rowland Hill's Brigade, 9 November, 1812. In 1813 he married Charlotte, daughter of the Rev. John Douglas, D.D., sometime Fellow of Magdalene College, Oxford. Retiring from the service in 1815, he practised as a Surgeon in Colchester for a period of nineteen years, removing in 1834 to Liverpool, where he at once interested himself in his new surroundings and became in course of time a Town Councillor. He was chosen as a Member of a Committee to take in hand the drainage of Liverpool, in his attention to which duty, he contracted typhoid fever, and died 24 March, 1844.

Mr. Boutflower was described by his sons and nephews, as a man of great activity, and a general favourite with all his acquaintances. He was keenly interested in his professional work, and in this and beyond it his ambition was to be accounted a faithful public servant.